William A. Gladstone

Printed in the United States of America

Published by THOMAS PUBLICATIONS, P.O. Box 3031, Gettysburg, Pa. 17325

ISBN-O-939631-16-4

Photo Credits

Civil War Library and Museum - p. 99

Library Company of Philadelphia - p. 30 (bottom)

Miller's Photographic History of the Civil War - p. 61

Milwaukee Public Museum - pp. 72, 73, & 74

Museum of the U.S. Military Academy, West Point - p. 77

Thomas Publications - p. 98

Union League of Philadelphia - p. 10

U.S. Army Military History Institute - pp. 26, 27, 28, 32 (bottom), 48, 49, 53, 67, 68, 84, 96 & 97

TABLE OF CONTENTS

PREFACE

Bill Gladstone's *The United States Colored Troops, 1863-1867,* represents many years of research and collecting. Bill has turned those years of effort into a remarkable account of the nearly 200,000 black soldiers and sailors who participated in the military struggle to gain their own freedom.

Bill's skillful combination of photographs, prints, documents and other physical artifacts, mainly from his own extensive collection, graphically illustrates the black contribution to the story of the American Civil War. Some have called the story forgotten, but as Bill shows it was in truth ignored. Other capable historians have written of the United States Colored Troops, their portraits have been reproduced in countless books, but still they somehow have never figured in the popular conceptions of the war.

The United States Colored Troops makes a clear statement that black soldiers and sailors like their white counterparts went through bureaucratic entanglements. boring inaction, mindless fatigue duties and the terrors of combat. For blacks the American Civil War would be less than an end to slavery than the beginning of a new struggle. The black soldiers and sailors of that war set a gallant example of courage for the long struggle which lay ahead.

Michael J. McAfee
Newburgh, New York

ACKNOWLEDGMENTS

No book can be written without the help of others. I would like to thank many people for their help over the years in my search for information about the United States Colored Troops. Perhaps the first person for me to thank is Dudley Taylor Cornish, someone I don't know, for his book *The Sable Arm.* It was this book with his notes and bibliography that opened up a new world for me to explore.

I would like to thank Mike McAfee, Curator, Museum of the United States Military Academy, West Point for his guidance in my research.

Alan Aimone, Special Collections, Cadet Library, United States Military Academy who brought to my attention, information that became obvious after he told me where to find it.

Mike Musick, Old Army Branch, National Archives always was helpful in his vast knowledge of the files available to me.

At the U.S. Army Military History Institute, Mike Winey, Curator of Photo and Prints made access to the photos easy. Dr. Richard Sommers, Archivist and historian brought to my attention many areas of information novices such as myself would not have known. John Sloanaker, Librarian, made the library a user friendly source of information.

I wish to thank military historians such as Howard Madaus and Wendell Lang Jr. for their willingness to share their knowledge with me.

The more you delve into a particular field of interest the more you realize you don't know all about your field of interest. In the subject of the black soldier there is a tremendous amount of information available once you become aware of it. This is not always obvious to the researcher. I have found most of the curators of the various National Military Parks to be most helpful. This exchange of knowledge is freely given and most appreciative.

It is exciting to come across strongholds of information such as the Civil War Library and Museum in Philadelphia with its Director Russ Pritchard always willing to help.

I appreciate Richard J. Ferry for allowing me the use of his stencil of a black soldier. The Library Company of Philadelphia was most generous in allowing the use of their material.

Living in Westport, Connecticut, one would assume it is difficult to do research without traveling. The inter-library loan systems offered by the Westport Public Library and the cooperation of its staff has been a tremendous asset.

Finally I would like to thank David Teitelbaum who made it possible for me to live a particular lifestyle.

William A. Gladstone
Westport, Connecticut

"Let soldiers in war, be citizens in peace."

United States Colored Troops 1863-1867

From the American Revolution through the present, African-Americans have always volunteered to fight for their country, and the American Civil War (1861-1865) was no exception to this impressive record. When the Civil War began with the firing on Fort Sumter, African-Americans offered their services to both feuding factions. However, they were at first turned away by North and South for various reasons, not the least of which were race prejudice and the opinion it would be a short war.

The first official authorization to use black men in the military was the Second Confiscation and Militia Act of July 17, 1862. Section 12 authorized the president to receive into the service of the United States, for the purpose of constructing entrenchments or performing camp duty, or any labor, or any military or naval service for which they were found to be competent, persons of African descent, and provided that such persons should be enrolled and organized, under such regulations not inconsistent with the constitution and laws as the president might prescribe.

Section 15 of the act provided that persons of African descent [of any rank] who under this law shall be employed, shall receive $10 a month, and one ration, $3 of which monthly pay may be in clothes. White privates received $13 per month plus $3.50 in clothing allowance. By March 1865, the pay and bounty discrepancy was rectified.

Before the Emancipation Proclamation, January 1, 1863, five colored regiments were in service. They were the 1st South Carolina Volunteer Infantry Regiment (African Descent), the 1st, 2nd, and 3rd Regiment Louisiana Native Guards and the 1st Regiment Kansas Colored Infantry. The latter has the distinction of being the first colored troops to have engaged the enemy in October 1862 with a raiding party in Missouri. These five regiments were redesignated into U.S. Colored Troops, respectively becoming the 33rd, 73rd, 74th, 75th, and 79th (new) regiments U.S. Colored Troops.

Ironically, in order for black men to fight for their freedom, they would first have to fight for their right to join the military. The leading black abolitionist of the period, Frederick Douglass, felt by fighting for the cause the black man would earn his right to the citizenship that was denied to him: "Once let the black man get upon his person the brass letters 'U.S.,' let him get an eagle on his button, and a musket on his shoulder and bullets in his pocket, and there is no power on earth which can deny that he has earned the right to citizenship in the United States."

After the Emancipation Proclamation, permission was given to the Governor of Massachusetts to raise the first black regiment in the North. Permission was also given to raise the Corps d'Afrique under Major General Nathaniel P. Banks. These units were not part of the U.S. colored service until the Corps d'Afrique was later redesignated into regiments of the U.S. Colored Troops.

On May 22, 1863, the U.S. War Department issued General Order No. 143 establishing the Bureau of Colored Troops. This bureau was directly under the adjutant general's office, with Major C.W. Foster appointed chief with the title of assistant adjutant general.

BY THE PRESIDENT OF THE UNITED STATES OF AMERICA.

A Proclamation.

Whereas, on the twenty-second day of September, in the year of our Lord one thousand eight hundred and sixty-two, a proclamation was issued by the President of the United States, containing, among other things, the following, to wit:

"That on the first day of January, in the year of our Lord one thousand eight hundred and sixty-three, all persons held as slaves within any State or designated part of a State, the people whereof shall then be in rebellion against the United States, shall be then, thenceforward, and forever, free; and the Executive government of the United States, including the military and naval authority thereof, will recognize and maintain the freedom of such persons, and will do no act or acts to repress such persons, or any of them, in any efforts they may make for their actual freedom.

"That the Executive will, on the first day of January aforesaid, by proclamation, designate the States and parts of States, if any, in which the people thereof, respectively, shall then be in rebellion against the United States; and the fact that any State, or the people thereof, shall on that day be in good faith represented in the Congress of the United States, by members chosen thereto at elections wherein a majority of the qualified voters of such State shall have participated, shall, in the absence of strong countervailing testimony, be deemed conclusive evidence that such State, and the people thereof, are not then in rebellion against the United States."

Now, therefore, I, ABRAHAM LINCOLN, PRESIDENT OF THE UNITED STATES, by virtue of the power in me vested as commander-in-chief of the army and navy of the United States, in time of actual armed rebellion against the authority and government of the United States, and as a fit and necessary war measure for suppressing said rebellion, do, on this first day of January, in the year of our Lord one thousand eight hundred and sixty-three, and in accordance with my purpose so to do, publicly proclaimed for the full period of one hundred days from the day first above mentioned, order and designate as the States and parts of States wherein the people thereof, respectively, are this day in rebellion against the United States, the following, to wit: ARKANSAS, TEXAS, LOUISIANA, (except the Parishes of St. Bernard, Plaquemines, Jefferson, St. John, St. Charles, St. James, Ascension, Assumption, Terre Bonne, Lafourche, St. Mary, St. Martin, and Orleans, including the City of New Orleans,) MISSISSIPPI, ALABAMA, FLORIDA, GEORGIA, SOUTH CAROLINA, NORTH CAROLINA, AND VIRGINIA, (except the forty-eight counties designated as West Virginia, and also the counties of Berkeley, Accomac, Northampton, Elizabeth City, York, Princess Ann, and Norfolk, including the cities of Norfolk and Portsmouth,) and which excepted parts are for the present left precisely as if this proclamation were not issued.

And by virtue of the power and for the purpose aforesaid, I do order and declare that all persons held as slaves within said designated States and parts of States are and henceforward shall be free; and that the Executive government of the United States, including the military and naval authorities thereof, will recognize and maintain the freedom of said persons.

And I hereby enjoin upon the people so declared to be free to abstain from all violence, unless in necessary self-defence; and I recommend to them that, in all cases when allowed, they labor faithfully for reasonable wages.

And I further declare and make known that such persons, of suitable condition, will be received into the armed service of the United States, to garrison forts, positions, stations, and other places, and to man vessels of all sorts in said service.

And upon this act, sincerely believed to be an act of justice warranted by the Constitution upon military necessity, I invoke the considerate judgment of mankind and the gracious favor of Almighty God.

In witness whereof I have hereunto set my hand and caused the seal of the United States to be affixed.

[L. S.] Done at the CITY OF WASHINGTON this first day of January, in the year of our Lord one thousand eight hundred and sixty-three, and of the Independence of the United States of America the eighty-seventh.

By the President: Abraham Lincoln

William H Seward Secretary of State.

A true copy, with the autograph signatures of the President and the Secretary of State.

Jno. G. Nicolay
Priv. Sec. to the President.

Courtesy of *The Union League of Philadelphia.*

The bureau was responsible for recruiting colored soldiers, commissioning officers to command them, organizing regiments, and maintaining their records. The first regiment of the U.S. Colored Troops was mustered into the federal service at Washington, D.C., on June 30, 1863. The last regiment, the 125th, was not mustered out of service until December 1867.

Fourteen states raised volunteer units under their state designations eventually to be redesignated as U.S. Colored Troops. These segregated regiments were commanded almost exclusively by white officers. Three states raised colored regiments that maintained their state designation: Connecticut, Louisiana, and Massachusetts. By the end of the war, 178,975 enlisted men served in the U.S. Army as members of the U.S. Colored Troops. Another 9,695 black men served in the U.S. Navy.

These soldiers served their country in 135 infantry regiments, six cavalry regiments, 12 regiments of heavy artillery and 10 batteries of light artillery (see Appendix I). They fought in 39 major engagements and 410 lesser actions. Their record is one of valor, determination, and sacrifices.

The history of the African-American soldier in the Civil War involves more than the plight of the soldier, although he certainly is the key figure. The black soldier's participation was due to the efforts of both the white and colored man, politicians, Congress, military and religious leaders, abolitionists, and just plain folks of the nation. And as the number of colored soldiers increased, their participation expanded in the war. For most soldiers—North or South—the war was over with the surrenders of Lee and Johnston, but not for those of the U.S. Colored Troops. The last colored regiment was mustered out of service in December 1867, one and a half years after the war was over.

The Emancipation Proclamation (left) not only freed the slaves in rebellious states, but allowed them to serve in the armed services of the United States: "such persons, of suitable condition, will be received into the armed service of the United States, to garrison forts, positions, stations, and other places, and to man vessels of all sorts in said service."

In The Beginning

"Once let the black man get upon his person the brass letters 'US,' let him get an eagle on his button and a musket on his shoulder and bullets in his pockets and there is no power on earth which can deny that he has earned the right to citizenship in the United States."

— **Frederick Douglass**

"Once let the black man get upon his person the brass letters 'US,'

let him get an eagle on his button

and a musket on his shoulder

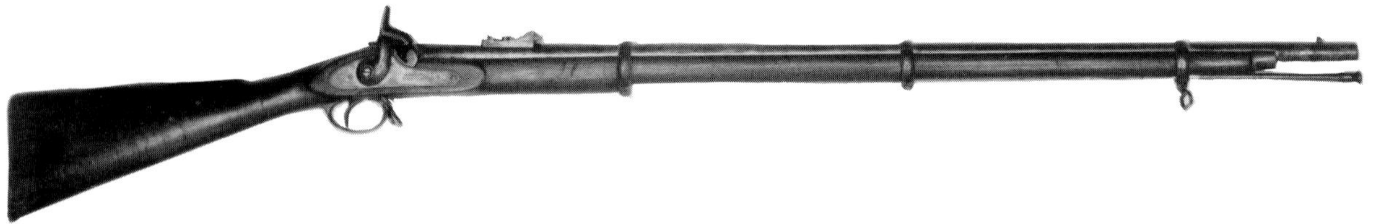

and bullets in his pockets

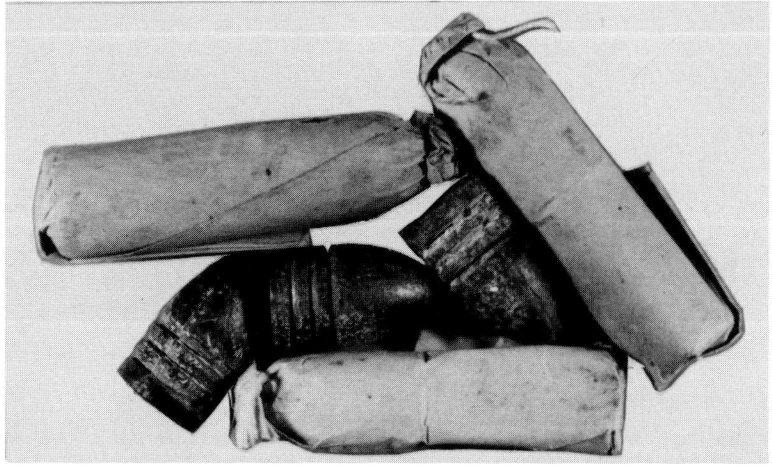

and there is no power on earth which can deny that he has earned the right to citizenship in the United States."

Before the Emancipation Proclamation was issued on January 1, 1863, five colored regiments had been formed. They were the 1st South Carolina Infantry Regiment (African Descent), the 1st, 2nd, and 3rd Louisiana Native Guards and the 1st Kansas Colored Infantry.

With the firing of the first shot on Fort Sumter, black men wanted to fight for their cause—volunteering to fight for the South as well as the North. Neither the Federal nor Confederate governments felt they wanted the colored man to be uniformed and armed. This *carte de visite* was sold in 1862 and had a copyright from Massachusetts. The painting was by W. M. Hunt.

Price Five Cents.

THE

UNITED STATES

CONSCRIPTION

LAW

OF

1863.

OFFICIAL AND COMPLETE

NEW YORK:
JAMES W. FORTUNE, PUBLISHER,
No. 102 CENTRE STREET.

The greatest single force in the progress of the colored soldier was the adoption of national conscription in March 1863. This act had no racial restrictions.

The political cartoonist Thomas Nast depicted the Colored Volunteer in 1863. Men of all wars trained with broomsticks and other forms of make-believe weapons.

General Order No. 143 authorized the formation of the Bureau of United States Colored Troops. This order officially began the recognition of the black soldier in the U. S. Army. Men became part of the U. S. Colored Troops three ways: redesignation of state volunteer regiments, redesignation of the Corps d'Afrique, and via the draft, enlistments, or as substitutes.

GENERAL ORDERS,
No. 143.

WAR DEPARTMENT,
ADJUTANT GENERAL'S OFFICE
Washington, May 22, 1863

I. A Bureau is established in the Adjutant General's Office for the record of all matters relating to the organization of Colored Troops. An officer will be assigned to the charge of the Bureau, with such number of clerks as may be designated by the Adjutant General.

II. Three or more field officers will be detailed as Inspectors to supervise the organization of colored troops at such points as may be indicated by the War Department in the Northern and Western States.

III. Boards will be convened at such posts as may be decided upon by the War Department to examine applicants for commissions to command colored troops, who, on application to the Adjutant General, may receive authority to present themselves to the board for examination.

IV. No persons shall be allowed to recruit for colored troops except specially authorized by the War Department; and no such authority will be given to persons who have not been examined and passed by a board; nor will such authority be given any one person to raise more than one regiment.

V. The reports of Boards will specify the grade of commission for which each candidate is fit, and authority to recruit will be given in accordance. Commissions will be issued from the Adjutant General's Office when the prescribed number of men is ready for muster into service.

VI. Colored troops may be accepted by companies, to be afterwards consolidated in battalions and regiments by the Adjutant General. The regiments will be numbered *seriatim*, in the order in which they are raised, the numbers to be determined by the Adjutant General. They will be designated: "— Regiment of U. S. Colored Troops."

VII. Recruiting stations and depots will be established by the Adjutant General as circumstances shall require, and officers will be detailed to muster and inspect the troops.

VIII. The non-commissioned officers of colored troops may be selected and appointed from the best men of their number in the usual mode of appointing non-commissioned officers. Meritorious commissioned officers will be entitled to promotion to higher rank if they prove themselves equal to it.

IX. All personal applications for appointments in colored regiments, or for information concerning them, must be made to the Chief of the Bureau; all written communications should be addressed to the Chief of the Bureau, to the care of the Adjutant General.

BY ORDER OF THE SECRETARY OF WAR:

E D Townsend

E.D. Townsend
Assistant Adjutant General.

Recruitment poster, circa 1863, circulated by the Supervisory Committee for Recruiting Colored Regiments, Philadelphia, Pa. Note that the word "colored" was not included, despite its intended audience.

Camp William Penn was located eight miles north of Philadelphia in Cheltanham Township. In its beginning the soldiers lived in tents, but by December 1863, wooden barracks had been erected.

Lieutenant Colonel Louis Wagner commanded Camp William Penn during its activation from June 1863 to May 1865.

In Philadelphia, the Supervisory Committee for Recruiting Colored Regiments was given permission by Secretary of War Edwin M. Stanton to raise three regiments of colored troops at Camp William Penn in Cheltanham Township. These became the 3rd, 6th, and 8th U. S. Colored Troops. This Supervisory Committee was founded by the Union League of Philadelphia.

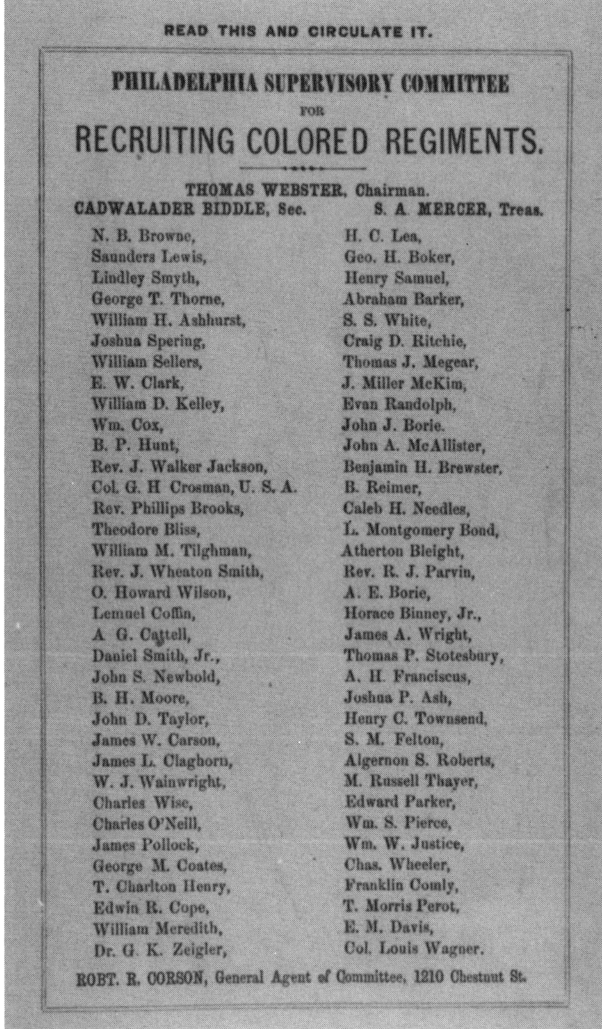

READ THIS AND CIRCULATE IT.

PHILADELPHIA SUPERVISORY COMMITTEE
FOR
RECRUITING COLORED REGIMENTS.

THOMAS WEBSTER, Chairman.
CADWALADER BIDDLE, Sec. S. A. MERCER, Treas.

N. B. Browne,	H. C. Lea,
Saunders Lewis,	Geo. H. Boker,
Lindley Smyth,	Henry Samuel,
George T. Thorne,	Abraham Barker,
William H. Ashhurst,	S. S. White,
Joshua Spering,	Craig D. Ritchie,
William Sellers,	Thomas J. Megear,
E. W. Clark,	J. Miller McKim,
William D. Kelley,	Evan Randolph,
Wm. Cox,	John J. Borie.
B. P. Hunt,	John A. McAllister,
Rev. J. Walker Jackson,	Benjamin H. Brewster,
Col. G. H Crosman, U. S. A.	B. Reimer,
Rev. Phillips Brooks,	Caleb H. Needles,
Theodore Bliss,	L. Montgomery Bond,
William M. Tilghman,	Atherton Bleight,
Rev. J. Wheaton Smith,	Rev. R. J. Parvin,
O. Howard Wilson,	A. E. Borie,
Lemuel Coffin,	Horace Binney, Jr.,
A. G. Cattell,	James A. Wright,
Daniel Smith, Jr.,	Thomas P. Stotesbury,
John S. Newbold,	A. H. Franciscus,
B. H. Moore,	Joshua P. Ash,
John D. Taylor,	Henry C. Townsend,
James W. Carson,	S. M. Felton,
James L. Claghorn,	Algernon S. Roberts,
W. J. Wainwright,	M. Russell Thayer,
Charles Wise,	Edward Parker,
Charles O'Neill,	Wm. S. Pierce,
James Pollock,	Wm. W. Justice,
George M. Coates,	Chas. Wheeler,
T. Charlton Henry,	Franklin Comly,
Edwin R. Cope,	T. Morris Perot,
William Meredith,	E. M. Davis,
Dr. G. K. Zeigler,	Col. Louis Wagner.

ROBT. R. CORSON, General Agent of Committee, 1210 Chestnut St.

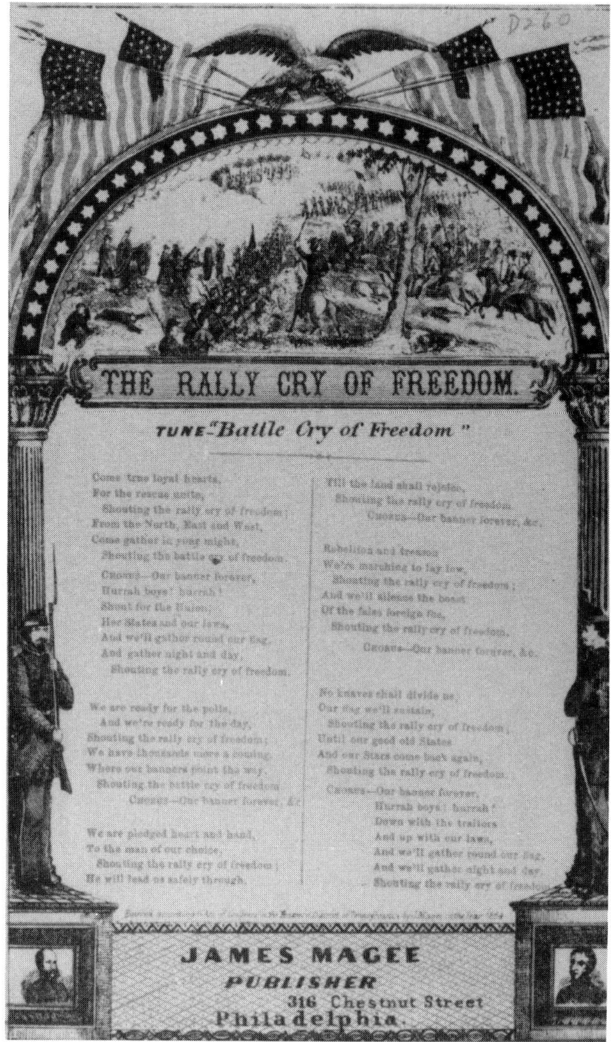

One of the rallying songs for the U. S. Colored Troops. Some of the colored regiments had distinct songs and music.

Marching Song of the 1st Arkansas
Words: Capt. Linley Miller
Music: John Brown's Body
The 1st Arkansas Infantry (African Descent) was redesignated to 46th U.S. Colored Troops.
The Second Louisiana*
Words: George H. Boker
Music: The Charge of the Light Brigade
The 2nd Louisiana Native Guards was eventually redesignated to 74th U.S. Colored Troops.

*Also known as the Black Regiment.

54th Regiment Massachusetts Infantry (Colored)
Give Us a Flag
Words: Unknown member of Company A
Music: Hoist up the Flag
9th U.S. Colored Troops
Negro Battle Hymn, "They Look Like Men of War"
107th U.S. Colored Troops
Doggerel, Captain Fiddler's Come to Town
Words: 13-year-old drummer boy
Music: Yankee Doodle

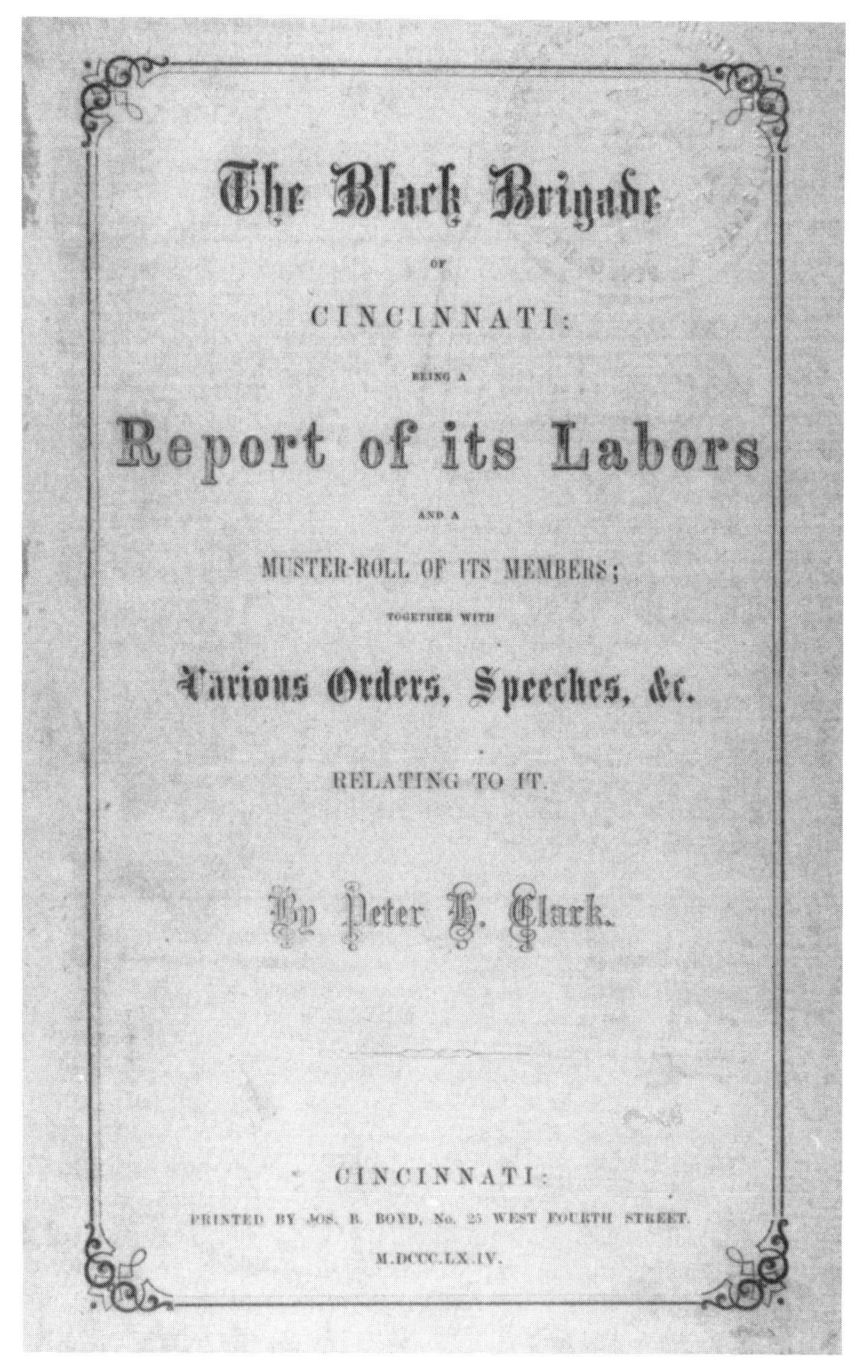

The Black Brigade

OF

CINCINNATI:

BEING A

Report of its Labors

AND A

MUSTER-ROLL OF ITS MEMBERS;

TOGETHER WITH

Various Orders, Speeches, &c.

RELATING TO IT.

By Peter H. Clark.

CINCINNATI:

PRINTED BY JOS. B. BOYD, No. 25 WEST FOURTH STREET.

M.DCCC.LX.IV.

The first appearance of the Negro in military operations occurred in September 1862 in Cincinnati, Ohio, at the time of the threatened invasion by Confederate General John Hunt Morgan. A so-called Black Brigade of three regiments was then organized, and assigned to duty in constructing the fortifications and earthworks about Cincinnati. These men gave their services voluntarily, but were unarmed and without uniforms. Their organization, such as it was, existed for only three weeks, and had no connections with the movement for enlisting colored troops.

The Officers

In May 1862, Union Major General David Hunter raised the first black regiment, the 1st South Carolina Volunteer Infantry (African Descent). This was a regiment of former slaves; many were impressed into service. The Lincoln government would not authorize the regiment at that time—May 1862—and all but one company was disbanded.

Later, Major General Rufus Saxton was given government authorization to arm, uniform, equip, and receive into the service of the United States such number of volunteers of African descent not exceeding 5,000. They maintained the same regimental identification—1st South Carolina Infantry—until they were redesignated the 33rd United States Colored Troops on February 4, 1864.

Between September and November 1862, Major General Benjamin Butler called on the free colored militia of Louisiana to enroll in the Volunteer force of the Union. The militia became the 1st, 2nd and 3rd Louisiana Native Guards. These regiments were redesignated the 1st 2nd, and 3rd Infantry Regiments, Corps d'Afrique, and later as the 73rd, 74th and 75th Regiments, U.S. Colored Troops.

Martin R. Delany was commissioned a major in the 104th U. S. Colored Troops on February 26, 1865. He was sent to the Department of the South to aid General Saxton in the recruitment and the organization of the 104th and 105th U. S. Colored Troops. The 104th was organized in Beaufort, South Carolina, to serve three years. The 105th failed to complete its organization. Major Delaney has been given the distinction of being the first black staff officer in the United States military, although Alexander T. Augusta, surgeon of the 7th U. S. Colored Troops, held a commission dated October 2, 1863, and was made brevet lieutenant colonel March 13, 1865.

Brevet Lieutenant Colonel Alexander T. Augusta was born in Norfolk, Virginia, in March 1825. He was graduated from the Trinity Medical College of the University of Toronto in 1856. During the Civil War, he was appointed surgeon of the 7th U. S. Colored Troops. His commission—the equivalent of a major—was dated October 2, 1863. Promoted to brevet lieutenant colonel on March 13, 1865, he thereby became the highest ranking black, officer in the Civil War era. Augusta was on detached duty at the Camp for Colored Persons while retaining his formal affiliation with the 7th U. S. Colored Troops. After the war, he saw service with the Freedman's Bureau.

Surgeon Augusta was the examining physician for this enlistee in the 33rd U. S. Colored Troops. The 33rd was formerly the 1st South Carolina before it was redesignated. This was the first black regiment on the Union side during the Civil War.

VOLUNTEER ENLISTMENT.

STATE OF South Carolina TOWN OF Beaufort

I, Madison Hilton, born in [illegible], in the State of South Carolina, aged [illegible] years, and by occupation a [illegible], Do hereby acknowledge to have volunteered this [illegible] day of May, 1865, to serve as a **Soldier** in the **Army of the United States of America**, for the period of *THREE YEARS*, unless sooner discharged by proper authority: Do also agree to accept such bounty, pay, rations, and clothing, as are or may be, established by law for volunteers. And I, Madison Hilton, do solemnly swear, that I will bear true faith and allegiance to the **United States of America**, and that I will serve them honestly and faithfully against all their enemies or opposers whomsoever; and that I will observe and obey the orders of the President of the United States, and the orders of the officers appointed over me, according to the Rules and Articles of War.

Sworn and subscribed to, at Beaufort S.C.
this 4th day of May 1865. } Madison his mark Hilton
Before [illegible]
Capt. 33rd U.S.C.T.

I CERTIFY, ON HONOR, That I have carefully examined the above-named Volunteer, agreeably to the General Regulations of the Army, and that, in my opinion, he is free from all bodily defects and mental infirmity, which would in any way disqualify him from performing the duties of a soldier.

A. T. Augusta
Surgeon 7th U.S.C.T.
EXAMINING SURGEON.

I CERTIFY, ON HONOR, That I have minutely inspected the Volunteer Madison Hilton previously to his enlistment, and that he was entirely sober when enlisted; that, to the best of my judgment and belief, he is of lawful age; and that, in accepting him as duly qualified to perform the duties of an able-bodied soldier, I have strictly observed the Regulations which govern the recruiting service. This soldier has Blk. eyes, Blk. hair, Black complexion, is [illegible] feet — inches high.

[illegible]
Capt. 33 Regiment of U.S.C. Volunteers,
RECRUITING OFFICER.

(A. G. O. No. 74 & 76.)

Certificate for the Signature of the Mustering Officer, Commissary, or Assistant Commissary of Musters, as the case may be.

Mustered into the service of the United States, for three years or during the war, from date of enlistment, in Co. ___ Regiment of ___ Volunteers, on the ___ day of ___, 186_, at ___ and credited to ___ Ward, (or Sub-district,) in the Town of ___, in the County of ___ th Congressional District, in the State of ___

Bounty paid at time of Muster-in:
U. S. Bounty,
Local Bounty,

African-American Surgeons During the Civil War

Anderson R. Abbott
Alexander T. Augusta, 7th U. S. Colored Troops
John V. DeGrasse (assistant surgeon), 35th U.S. Colored Troops, cashiered
William B. Ellis
William C. Powell, 127th U. S. Colored Troops
Charles B. Purvis
John Rapier
Alephus Tucker

(Abbott, Ellis, Purvis, Rapier, and Tucker probably performed their duties in hospitals as contract surgeons.)

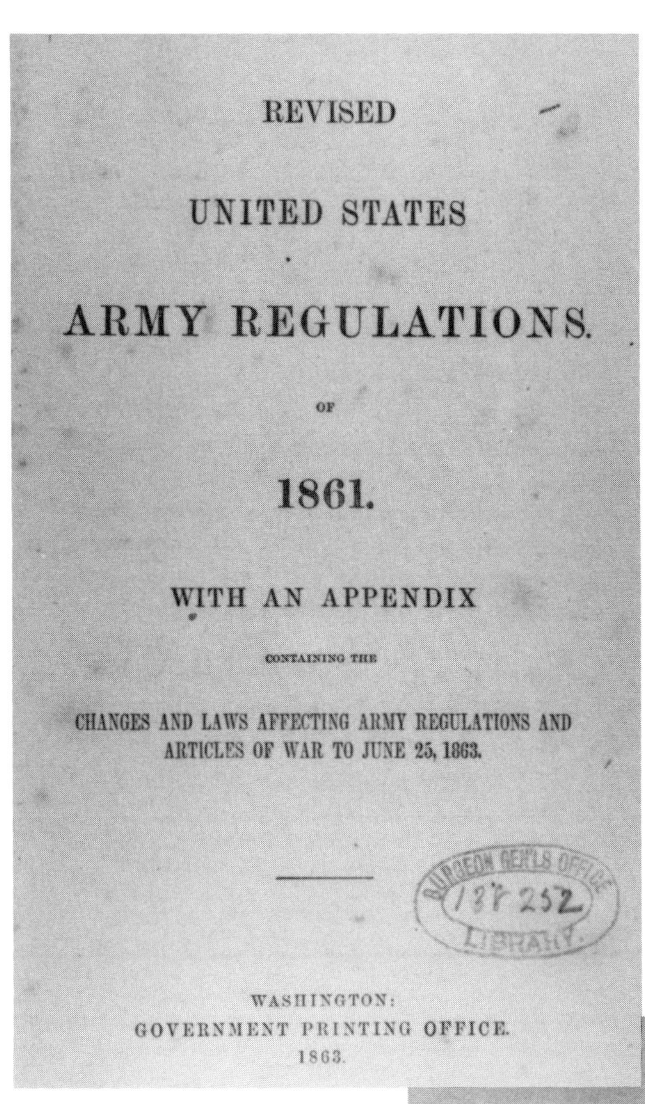

REVISED

UNITED STATES

ARMY REGULATIONS.

OF

1861.

WITH AN APPENDIX

CONTAINING THE

CHANGES AND LAWS AFFECTING ARMY REGULATIONS AND ARTICLES OF WAR TO JUNE 25, 1863.

WASHINGTON:
GOVERNMENT PRINTING OFFICE.
1863.

This copy of *United States Army Regulations* belonged to Alexander T. Augusta. It is signed "A.T. Augusta, M.B. Surgeon 7' Rgt U.S.C.T." Note that "M.B." stands for "Medicinae Baccalaures" or Bachelor of Medicine. Identified artifacts belonging to the highest ranking African- American officer—or to any other African-American officers—are very rare.

First Sergeant Stephen Swails, Company F, 54th Massachusetts Infantry Regiment, was the first black soldier to break the color barrier of commissioned officers in Massachusetts regiments. Sergeant Swails was cited for his "coolness, bravery, and efficiency" during his participation in the Battle of Olustee, February 20, 1864. He was commissioned a second lieutenant in the 54th Massachusetts on March 11, 1864, by Governor John Andrew. However, the War Department would not give him a discharge to receive his commission, which he eventually received April 28, 1865.

Two other sergeants from the 54th were commissioned second lieutenants: Frank M. Welch and Peter Vogelsang. They were also made first lieutenants within a month of their promotions. Lieutenant Welch continued his military career after the war with the Connecticut National Guard. As a major he became the highest ranking colored officer.

Second Lieutenant Peter Vogelsang served with the 54th Massachusetts Infantry Regiment. The 54th Massachusetts was the first colored regiment recruited in the North. All of the other regiments in service at the time were from the South or the border states. The 54th was organized at Camp Meigs, Readville, Massachusetts, from March 30 to May 13, 1863, to serve three years, but they were mustered out of service August 20, 1865. The 54th Massachusetts participated in battles at James Island, Fort Wagner, Honey Hill, and Boykins Mill in South Carolina and at Olustee, Florida.

Second Lieutenant John F. Shorter

Second Lieutenant William H. Dupree

Governor John Andrew commissioned eight sergeants as officers in the 55th Massachusetts Infantry Regiment. Only three of these men were mustered in as officers; the others were mustered out of the regiment. Second Lieutenant John F. Shorter and Second Lieutenant William H. Dupree were commissioned at that rank. James Monroe Trotter was the third of the sergeants who was commissioned second lieutenant. These sergeants distinguished themselves in the field. Dupree was commissioned in May 1864, Shorter in March 1864, and Trotter in April 1864, but were not mustered into service as officers until some time later. Dupree received his commission June 21, 1865, Shorter received his commission July 1, 1865 and Trotter received his commission June 7, 1865.

James Monroe Trotter was born the son of a slave in Grand Gulf, Mississippi, on November 8, 1842. He enlisted as a private June 11, 1863, in Company K, 55th Regiment Massachusetts Volunteer Infantry (Colored). Promoted to sergeant major of the regiment, he became one of the three black soldiers later commissioned as officers in the 55th Massachusetts when he was made a second lieutenant June 7, 1865. He became the first black music historian by writing the epochal 508-page *Music and Some Highly Musical People.* In 1888, President Grover Cleveland appointed him as recorder of deeds in Washington, D.C., at that time the highest position a black man had held in the United States—replacing Frederick Douglass.

More than 100 African-American officers served during the Civil War, most of them in the 1st, 2nd, and 3rd Louisiana Native Guards. One of them was this unidentified officer.

The building and banner of the Free Military School for White Applicants to Command Colored Troops, a forerunner of Officers Candidate School, is shown at 1210 Chestnut Street, Philadelphia, Pennsylvania.

"An Officer's Creed"

This illustration expresses the opinion of those in charge of the Free Military School and the caliber of white officers they were seeking. The quality of these white officers is self-evident—thirteen of the 7,122 officers in the United States Colored Troops were awarded the Medal of Honor.

NO PERSON IS WANTED as an Officer in a Colored Regiment who "feels that he is making a sacrifice in accepting a position in a Colored Regiment," or who desires the place simply for higher rank and pay. It is the aim of those having this organization in charge to make Colored Troops equal to the best of White Troops, in Drill, Discipline and Officers. It is more than possible that Colored Troops will hereafter form no inconsiderable portion of the permanent army of the United States, and it should be the aim of every officer of Colored Troops to make himself and his men fit for such an honorable position.

It can be no "sacrifice" to any man to command in a service which gives Liberty to Slaves, and Manhood to Chattels, as well as Soldiers to the Union.

Colonel John H. Taggart was the preceptor of the Free Military School, which was operational from December 26, 1863, to September 15, 1864. When it closed, Taggart opened another school, this time requiring a fee, called "The United States Military School for Officers."

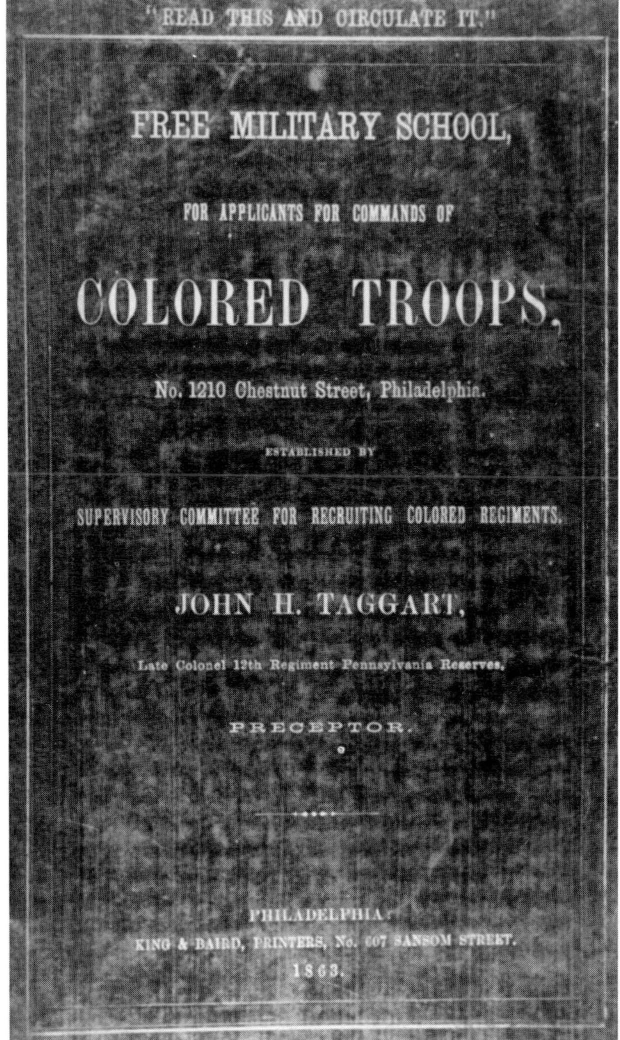

"READ THIS AND CIRCULATE IT."

FREE MILITARY SCHOOL,

FOR APPLICANTS FOR COMMANDS OF

COLORED TROOPS,

No. 1210 Chestnut Street, Philadelphia.

ESTABLISHED BY

SUPERVISORY COMMITTEE FOR RECRUITING COLORED REGIMENTS.

JOHN H. TAGGART,

Late Colonel 12th Regiment Pennsylvania Reserves,

PRECEPTOR.

PHILADELPHIA:
KING & BAIRD, PRINTERS, No. 607 SANSOM STREET.
1863.

This 1863 pamphlet was the first of two versions to be circulated; the second was dated 1864. The school was sponsored by the Union League of Philadelphia.

Black Chaplains in the Union Army*

Asher, Jeremiah, Baptist, 6th U.S. Colored Troops
Bowles, John R., Baptist, 55th Massachusetts Infantry (Colored)
Boyd, Francis A., Christian, 109th U.S. Colored Troops, appointment revoked
Harrison, Samuel, Congregational, 54th Massachusetts Infantry (Colored)
Hunter, William H., African Methodist Episcopal, 4th U.S. Colored Troops
Jackson, William, Baptist, 55th Massachusetts Infantry (Colored)
Leonard, Chauncey, Baptist, L'Ouverture Hospital, Alexandria, Virginia
Levere, George W., Congregational, 20th U.S. Colored Troops
Randolph, Benjamin F., Presbyterian, 26th U.S. Colored Troops
Stevens, David, African Methodist Episcopal, 36th U.S. Colored Troops
Turner, Henry M., 1st U.S. Colored Troops
Underdue, James, Baptist, 39th U.S. Colored Troops
Waring, William, Baptist, 102nd U.S. Colored Troops
White, Garland H., African Methodist Episcopal, 28th U.S. Colored Troops

* Redkey, Edwin, "Black Chaplains in the Union Army," *Civil War History*, Vol. XXXIII, No. 4, 1987, p. 350.

Jeremiah Asher
Died of disease in the service July 27, 1865.

John R. Bowles

Samuel Harrison

Colonel William B. Wooster, 29th Connecticut Volunteer Infantry (Colored)

The 29th Connecticut was a state Volunteer regiment whose identity was maintained throughout the war. Connecticut also raised a battalion of the 30th Regt. transferred to the 31st U.S.C.T. for they did not have enough men to fill the regiment.

The square on the reunion ribbon was the emblem for the 25th Army Corps. This was the first all-black army corps in the U.S. Army. The color was red to represent the First Division of the 25th Army Corps.

Officers of the 101st U.S. Colored Troops

The 101st Infantry Regiment U.S. Colored Troops was organized from September 17, 1864, to August 5, 1865, in Tennessee, to serve three years. It was composed of men unfit for service in the field, but able to perform ordinary fatigue and garrison duty, and of men transferred from other black regiments serving in the Department of the Cumberland incapacitated for services in the field. They participated in the Alabama battles of Scottsboro, Boyd's Station, and Madison Station. Ten of the enlisted men were killed and four were wounded. One officer was wounded and one missing.

If you look carefully at the officers in the photo, you will notice the second seated man from the right is missing a leg. The third standing man from the left seems to have an empty sleeve.

Readville April 9 1863

Col Lee,

Dear Sir,

I have asked the Governor to send for Tucker, Howard & Littlefield, in addition to those, whose names I gave him yesterday — Jones, Pope, Simpkins & Pond —.

Yours very truly

Robert G. Shaw

—

I have taken them in the order of your list, as I had no other guide to go by, & didn't get as far as Stevens.

Colonel Robert Gould Shaw, 54th Regiment, Massachusetts Volunteer Infantry (Colored), 25 years old, gave his life leading his men in the charge of Fort Wagner, South Carolina, on July 18, 1863. His death helped change the feelings of many who doubted the fighting capability of the colored soldier. Poems and songs were written on the valor of Shaw and his men.

One month before the regiment was mustered into service, Shaw requested from Colonel Francis L. Lee, 44th Regiment Massachusetts Volunteer Infantry, the following enlisted men: Corporal Charles E. Tucker, Company E; Acting Regimental Adjutant Willard Howard, Company D; Acting Regimental Adjutant Henry W. Littlefield, Company D; Sergeant Edward L. Jones, Company F; Corporal George Pope, Company F; Sergeant William H. Simpkins, Company F; and Sergeant Albert Pond, Company C. All except Pond were transferred to the 54th Regiment. Pond had been wounded at Rawle's Mill, which may be the reason he was not transferred.

Many of these requested men fell or were wounded in the Battle of Fort Wagner. Tucker became a captain in Company H and was wounded at Fort Wagner. Howard became a captain in Company I and was discharged on the expiration of his term. Littlefield became a first lieutenant and was wounded at the Battle of Olustee, Florida. Jones became a captain in Company D, was wounded at Fort Wagner, and resigned on account of wounds. Pope became a lieutenant colonel, was wounded at Fort Wagner, and was discharged at the expiration of his term. Simpkins became a captain in Company K and was killed at Fort Wagner.

"Storming Fort Wagner" depicts Colonel Robert Gould Shaw leading his men of the 54th Massachusetts charging the ramparts, July 18, 1863. This young abolitionist reached the ramparts, turned and shouted to his men, "Onward fifth-fourth!" That was the last thing he said, for he was felled by a ball in the chest. The rebels were so irate that colored soldiers were led by a white officer they stripped his body of his uniform and threw him in a common grave with his men on top of him.

The Soldiers

VOLUNTEER ENLISTMENT.

STATE OF Ark. COUNTY OF Sebastian

I, Joseph Logan born in Johnson County in the State of Arkansas aged Twenty three years, and by occupation a Laborer Do Hereby Acknowledge to have volunteered this nineteenth day of October 1863, to serve as a SOLDIER, in the Army of the United States, for the period of THREE YEARS, unless sooner discharged by proper authority: Do also agree to accept such bounty, pay, rations and clothing, as are, or may be established by law for colored volunteers.

And I, Joseph Logan do solemnly swear that I will bear true faith and allegiance to the United States of America, and that I will serve them honestly and faithfully against all their enemies or opposers whomsoever; and that I will observe and obey the orders of the President of the United States, and the orders of the officers appointed over me, according to the Rules and Articles of War.

Sworn and subscribed to, at Ft. Smith ark
this 19th day of October 1863
Before John Hayes Jr 2nd Lieut
Recruiting 2nd Kas. colored vols

his
Joseph X Logan
mark

I CERTIFY, ON HONOR, That I have carefully examined the above named Volunteer agreeable to the General Regulations of the Army, and that in my opinion he is free from all bodily defects and mental infirmity, which would in any way disqualify him from performing the duties of a soldier.

A. D. Tenney Asst. Sur. 1st Ks. Col. Inf.
EXAMINING SURGEON.

I CERTIFY, ON HONOR, That I have minutely inspected the Volunteer, previously to his enlistment, and that he was entirely sober when he enlisted; that, to the best of my judgment and belief, he is of lawful age; and that, in accepting him as duly qualified to perform the duties of an able-bodied soldier, I have strictly observed the Regulations which govern the Recruiting Service. This soldier has black eyes, black hair, black complexion, is five feet seven inches high.

John Hayes Jr 2nd Lieut
2nd Regiment of Kas. Colored Volunteers.
RECRUITING OFFICER.

The enlistment form did not have the word "colored" as part of its text—thus the word had to be inserted, as shown in this Volunteer Enlistment for Joseph Logan, who joined the 2nd Kansas Colored Infantry. At this time, October 1863, there was no bounty for colored soldiers; the pay was less than for white soldiers and their three-dollar clothing allowance was deducted from their ten-dollar monthly pay. Like many laborers of the time, Logan was unable two write his name and had to make his mark "X". The 2nd Kansas Colored Infantry was later redesignated the 83rd Regiment United States Colored Troops (new).

Head Quarters
Camp Ullmann
May 28th 1863

Special Order }
No 11 }

Capt Thomas S. White
4th Regt U.S. Cols

So much of special order no 5 from these headquarters as relates to the limits of recruiting negroes at Boutte station is hereby revoked

You are hereby authorized to enlist negroes on any plantation this side of the Mississippi river. Should any person or persons interfere with your business you will report such person or persons immediately at these head=quarters. You will further more make a report in writing to these headquarters once every three days.

Quartermasters will furnish transportation for Capt White as he may require

By Command of
Col. A. B. Botsford
Comdg Camp
Geo. C. Getchell
Actg Asst Adjt Genl

Recruitment of Plantation Negroes

Union officials felt that the South was a great source of manpower for the military. By taking men away, it would also mean the South would not have access to this valuable resource. This Special Order, dated May 28, 1863, after the formation of the U.S. Colored Troops, would allow plantation Negroes to enlist in the Union Army. Anyone interfering with this order was to be reported immediately to headquarters at Camp Ullman.

"The Black Conscription" appeared on September 26, 1863, in *Punch*, a British periodical. This illustration was sold in *carte de visite* format. You may think it interesting that the artist of the *Punch* illustration is almost certainly John Tenniel, who did the original illustrations for *Alice in Wonderland* and *Through the Looking Glass.*

President Jefferson Davis was an early proponent of using slaves in any way necessary to win the war. As the war continued, Confederate leaders began to change their opinion about slaves in the Confederate army. General Patrick Cleburne voiced his favor. On January 11, 1865, General Robert E. Lee sanctioned the policy of arming slaves. The inevitable was coming—slaves would be armed. It came but too late.

Sergeant Major Charles Springer of the 107th U.S. Colored Troops organized in Louisville, Kentucky. The sergeant major is the highest ranking non-commissioned officer in an infantry regiment. Springer is wearing the regulation four-button fatigue coat (commonly called a sack coat), a non-commissioned officer's sash, a Model 1840 non-commissioned officer's sword, gauntlets, and a forage cap. His straight cuffless "stove pipe" trousers were made of sky-blue kersey with a one-and-a-half-inch stripe down the side of his pants. He has a black leather belt with a non-commissioned officer's buckle. His chevrons are those of the sergeant major.

Infantry Soldiers

This first sergeant serves with Company G, 77th U.S. Colored Troops, which was formerly the 5th Regiment Infantry, Corps d'Afrique. The first sergeant is the highest ranking non-commissioned officer in a company. He is wearing the 1840 non-commissioned officer's sword. In his left hand is a Hardee hat showing regimental numerals, company letter, and infantry bugle device. He has on a frock coat with a non-commissioned officer's brass shoulder scales. He is wearing a black leather belt with the oval "US" buckle. This sergeant's trousers are of sky-blue kersey with a one-and-a-half-inch stripe down the side. His chevrons are those of the first sergeant.

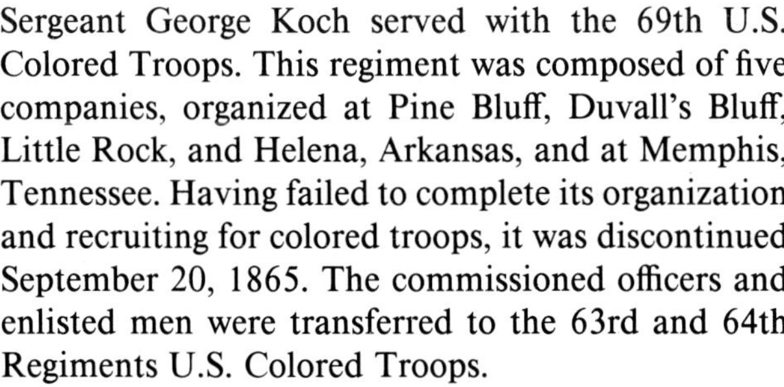

Sergeant George Koch served with the 69th U.S. Colored Troops. This regiment was composed of five companies, organized at Pine Bluff, Duvall's Bluff, Little Rock, and Helena, Arkansas, and at Memphis, Tennessee. Having failed to complete its organization and recruiting for colored troops, it was discontinued September 20, 1865. The commissioned officers and enlisted men were transferred to the 63rd and 64th Regiments U.S. Colored Troops.

Corporal Charlie Mguda is wearing the regulation frock coat and western-style hat. Also visible in the photograph are his oval "US" belt plate, black leather belt, percussion cap pouch, bayonet, and cartridge box shoulder sling with circular eagle plate.

Although the Conscription Act of March 1863 was interpreted to draft colored men, it was not until February 29, 1864, that the law was changed to specifically include the enrollment of blacks. Colored troops were recruited until April 29, 1865, after which there was no need for additional men.

Private Jesse Keepson, Company F, 108th Infantry Regiment, U.S. Colored Troops. Written on the reverse of the original photograph was "Hunted through the swamps a week by his master before he reached a boat. Performed his duty well—not very smart." Keepson is standing at attention with his Enfield rifled musket with fixed bayonet.

Private William Adams, Company F, 108th Infantry Regiment U.S. Colored Troops. This regiment was organized in Louisville, Kentucky, to serve three years. It participated in one major engagement at Owensboro, Kentucky, on August 27, 1864. Adams is standing at rest with his Enfield rifled musket.

This "dog tag," or identification disk, belonged to Private George Cudjo. The Canadian-born Cudjo was a 30-year-old farmer when he enlisted as a substitute for William Cooke of Brooklyn, New York, on August 19, 1864. Cudjo was mustered out of service November 7, 1865, at Brownsville, Texas. The brass disk was probably purchased from the regimental sutler, George H. Josselyn. On the face is "Abraham Lincoln, President U.S. War of 1861." The reverse reads "George Cudjo, Co. I, 31st USCT USA 1865."

The photo on the left in this piece of "before-and-after" propaganda identifies the barefoot young slave in his ragged clothing as "Jackson." Written on the back is: "As he appeared when he came into our lines." In the picture on the right he appears as a drummer in the 79th Infantry Regiment, U.S. Colored Troops. Written on the reverse of this image is: "As he appeared two weeks later."

The regiment was organized at Port Hudson, Louisiana, as the 7th Regiment Infantry, Corps d'Afrique, to serve three years. Its designation was later changed to the 79th Infantry Regiment, U.S. Colored Troops.

"Jackson" is wearing a frock coat, gloves and a black belt with a rectangular buckle. The snare drum is non-regulation, for it should have had its unit designation within an eagle design. The sling is of white webbing. The drum could have been a photographer's studio "prop."

There were a number of photographs of black men with the "before-and-after" theme. Usually, men appeared in one photo in ragged clothing and then neatly dressed in military uniform in a second photograph. This was intended to convey the belief that the government was saying, "Give us your ragged and poor and we will clothe, feed, dress and make soldiers out of them." Wearing gloves was a social distinction usually reserved for genteel white people. Being a soldier was a step toward citizenship.

This "before and after" 8 inch by 10 inch albumen photo adorned the wall of a proud family for many years after the war. The image on the left had the hair retouched on the photo itself. At this time, retouching the negatives was not done. The photo on the right was taken in a photographer's studio with a camp scene background. The term "albumen" is used because egg white was used in the processing of the paper.

The beginning of clinical and medical photography in the U.S. Army began with photographing the wounded in the Civil War. This culminated with the six-volume set of books called the *Medical and Surgical History of the War of the Rebellion.*

This *carte de visite* of a sergeant wearing a shell jacket was probably taken at an Army hospital, to show the results of having a hand amputated at the wrist. "Contr Phot. 1733" means this was a contributed photograph for this series.

Disease took an especially high toll of black troops. Whereas two white soldiers died of disease for every one who fell in battle or died of wounds, the ratio among black soldiers was roughly ten to one. While about one out of every ten white soldiers died of disease, roughly one in five black soldiers did. In Virginia during the closing months of the war, for example, the medical director of the Army of the James calculated that sickness struck four black soldiers for every white stricken and that black deaths from disease outnumbered white by seven to one.

Advertising Trade Cards

HELMBOLD'S FLUID EXTRACT of BUCHU,

THE GREAT TONIC DIURETIC AND INVIGORATOR.

HELMBOLD'S FLUID EXTRACT OF SARSAPARILLA,

The great blood purifier and beautifer of the complexion. One table spoonful added to a pint of water constitutes the Lisbon diet drink, and one bottle fully equals one gallon of syrup or decoction.

HELMBOLD'S ROSE WASH,

For external use, and to be used in connection with the Sarsaparilla and Buchu as per direction on wrapper.

H. T. HELMBOLD,

Drug & Chemical Warehouse,

594 BROADWAY, New York.

These four chromolitho trade cards are in a series by Helmbold's Fluid Extract of Buchu. There are about thirteen of these trade cards in this series. These are the same size as a *carte de visite*, 4 inches by 2 inches.

The band of the 107th Infantry Regiment, U.S. Colored Troops, was photographed November 18, 1865, at Fort Corcoran in Washington, D.C. These musicians were led by a white bandmaster. Very often the money for the instruments would be donated by the officers of the regiment. They have a matched set of "over-the-shoulder" saxhorns. The bandmaster is holding a bell-front cornet.

Shown are the Guard House and Guard of the 107th Infantry Regiment, U.S. Colored Troops, Fort Corcoran, Washington, D.C. The Guard Mount is at rest with their Springfield rifled muskets. Fort Corcoran, on the west side of the Potomac River, was one of the 68 forts and batteries defending the nation's capital.

EVIDENCE OF TITLE.

I, John S Gibbons, of Calvert County, Md., do solemnly swear that James E Shannon who has been enlisted in the 30th Regiment, U. S. Colored Troops, Co. K; is my slave for life; (his term of service expiring on the day of 186 ;) and that I became possessed of him by inheritance, in the month of January, eighteen hundred and fifty. And I do further swear that I have not purchased said slave from any person or persons disloyal to the Government of the United States, with the object of obtaining compensation for the same: and furthermore, that I have no agency for obtaining compensation for any person or persons but such as, to my knowledge, are loyal citizens of the United States.

John S. Gibbons

July 8th, 1864.

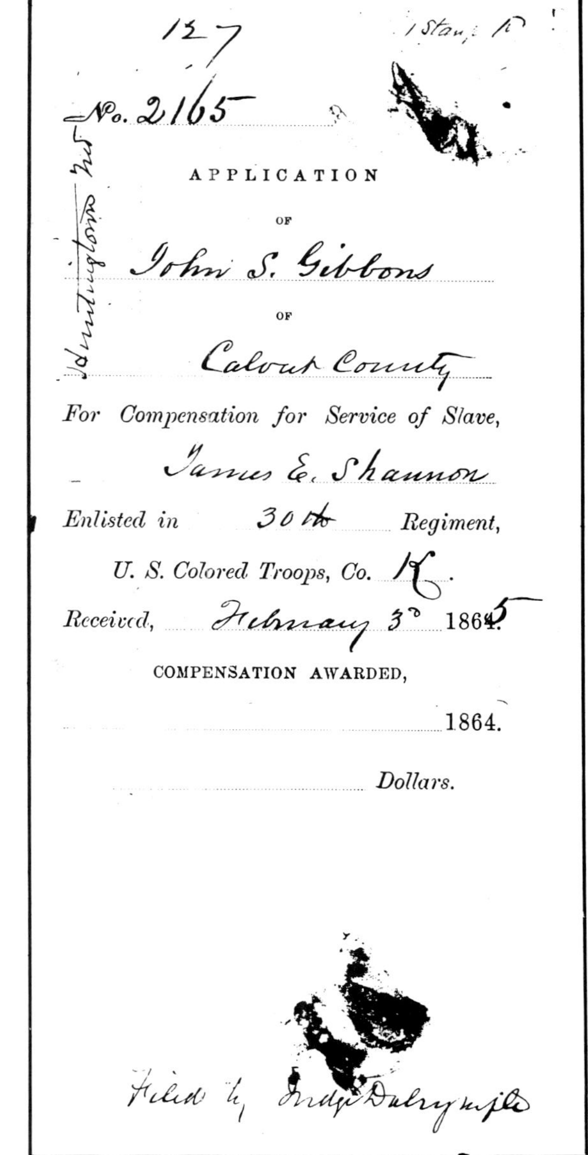

127 1 Stamp

No. 2165

Huntingtown Md

APPLICATION

OF

John S. Gibbons

OF

Calvert County

For Compensation for Service of Slave,

James E. Shannon

Enlisted in 30th Regiment,

U. S. Colored Troops, Co. K.

Received, February 3d 1865

COMPENSATION AWARDED,

1864.

Dollars.

Filed by Judge Dalrymple

This is an application for slave owner John S. Gibbons of Maryland to be compensated for having his slave, James E. Shannon, enlist in the 30th Infantry Regiment, U.S. Colored Troops.

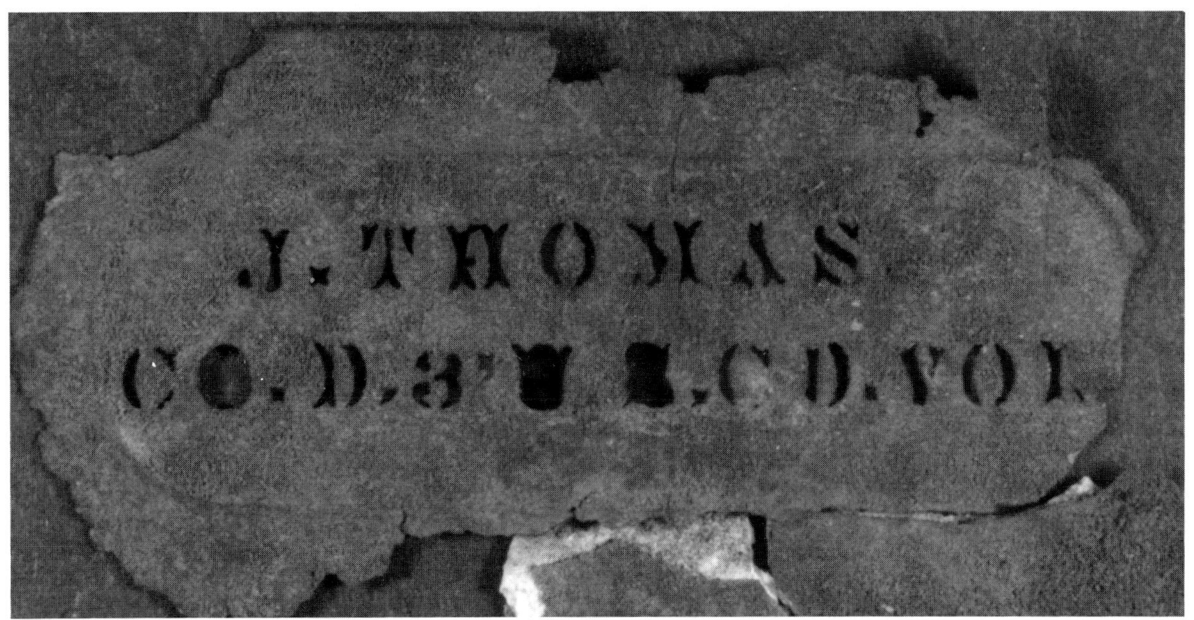

In a soldier's haversack one might find a brass stencil.

This is the identification stencil of John Thomas, Company D, 3rd U.S. Colored Volunteers (Troops). Pension records indicate he was a sergeant in Company D and was 5 feet 7 inches tall. Thomas was born in 1839 and was from Chester County, Pennsylvania, where he was a farmer. He died April 8, 1915.

In a soldier's pocket one might find a sutler's token.

This sutler's token from the 27th U.S. Colored Troops was found at Bermuda Hundred, Virginia.

The sutler was a civilian who sold necessities and alcohol to soldiers. They received their appointment for a period of three years by the Secretary of War. Some regiments had sutlers traveling with them in the field. Each payday the sutler would wait with the paymaster to settle their accounts with the soldiers.

It is very rare to find photographs in *carte de visite* format, or in any size, of colored soldiers and their ladies. This unidentified soldier is attributed to the 15th Infantry Regiment, U.S. Colored Troops.

The 15th U.S. Colored Troops was organized in Nashville, Tennessee. They participated in two battles: Nashville and Magnolia. They were mustered into service for three years December 2, 1863, and mustered out April 17, 1866.

Like most U.S. Colored Troops, the 10th Infantry Regiment was a three-year regiment. It participated in two engagements at Plymouth, North Carolina, as well as battles at Petersburg and Wilson's Wharf, Virginia. This is the winter encampment of the 10th U.S. Colored Troops at Fort Brady, Virginia, in 1864. The camp is laid out according to Army regulations. The stereo view was published and sold by the E. & H.T. Anthony Company.

The 1st Infantry Regiment, U.S. Colored Troops, was part of the 1st Brigade, 3rd Division, 18th Army Corps. They participated in the battles of Wilson's Wharf, Petersburg, Chapin's Farm, Fair Oaks, Fillmore, Town Creek, Wilmington and Warsaw. This photograph was taken on November 16, 1864.

This photograph was taken after the Battle of the Crater, (Seige of Petersburg) July 30, 1864. The soldier on guard duty could be from any of the 22 infantry regiments of the colored troops that participated in this battle. Brigadier General Ferrero's specially trained black troops were supposed to spearhead the assault on the crater. Generals Grant and Meade changed the order the day before the battle. It was felt public opinion would be against them if the attack was a failure and the black troops leading the attack could be considered as having been used as cannon fodder. The attack was a failure for other reasons and the outraged Confederates shot many of the colored troops from the rim of the crater after they had surrendered.

The soldier is standing at attention with his rifle and fixed bayonet.

Cavalry Soldiers, dismounted (left) and mounted (below).

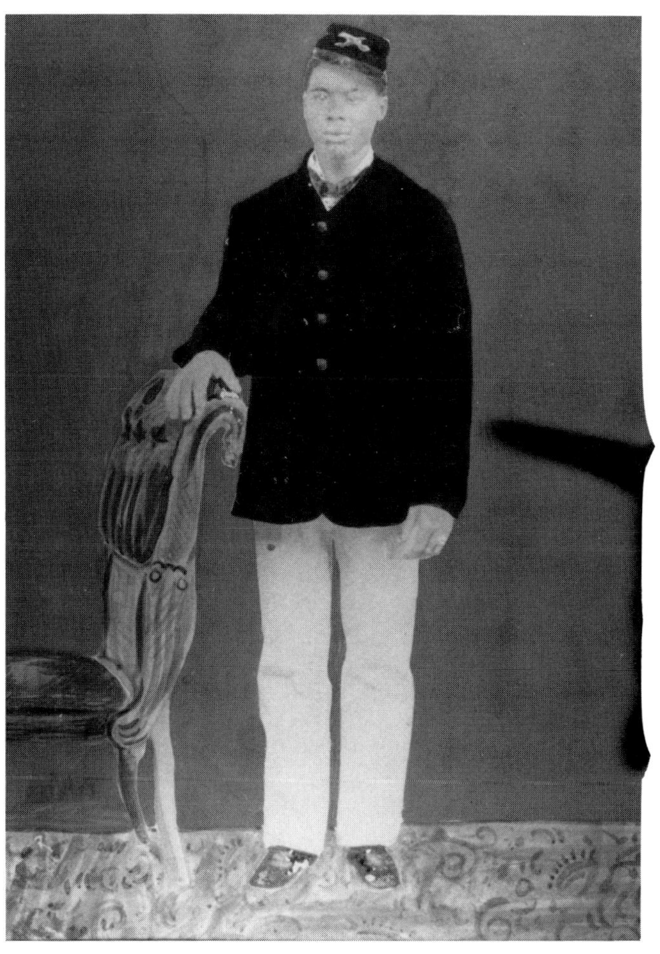

This is a non-professional, hand-tinted 8-inch by 10-inch wet plate, albumen photograph of a cavalry private in his four-button sack coat. The crossed sabers on his kepi are tinted in gold.

This is a cased outdoor scene, quarter plate ambrotype, of a mounted cavalry soldier wearing a shell jacket, with his saber drawn. An ambrotype is a collodion positive on glass.

Head Quarters 4th U.S.C.C.
Camp Parapet La. July 28/64

Instructions for the Guard.

The Officer of the Guard will be held strictly responsible for the Cleanness of the entire Camp. He will also see that his Guard as soon as relieved fires their muskets at the target. He will leave a bugler detailed with his Guard and will cause that he punctually calls the different calls, as per General Order No 12.

Reveille	5.30.	O'clock.
Sick Call,	5.45.	"
Breakfast Call	6.	"
Guard Mounting	7.	"
Drill Call	7.30	"
Recall	9.	"
Dinner	12	M.
Drill Call	4.30	P.M.
Recall	6.30	"
Dress Parade	7.	"
Supper immediately after parade,		
Tattoo.	8.30.	P.M
Taps,	9.	"

The Officer of the Guard will see that his Guard is kept clean. After retreat he ~~Guard~~ will see that their uniform is changed into blouses. He will not permit any man under his command to leave the Guard House except for their meals which they must do by relief.

The Officer of the Guard will be held strictly responsible for the enforcement of these Instructions. By not doing so he will be subject to a General Court Martial.

By Order of Lt Col
J. H. Alexander
O. C. Jackson
1st Lt and Acty Adjt

These instructions will be turned over to the New Officer of the Guard.

In camp, the commanding officer prescribed the hours of reveille, reports, roll calls, and so on. Above are the daily calls for the 4th United States Colored Cavalry. At this time the 4th Cavalry was stationed at Camp Parapet, New Orleans, Louisiana.

This regiment was originally organized as the 1st Cavalry Regiment, Corps d'Afrique, to serve three years. It was redesignated April 4, 1864. Its major engagement was the Battle of Clinton, Louisiana, on August 25, 1864. Three enlisted men were wounded in this engagement.

"An incident in the Battle of the Wilderness. The rebel Generals Bradley Johnson and E. Stuart taken to the rear by Negro cavalry, April 12, 1864," from *Frank Leslie's Illustrated Newspaper*, June 4, 1864. Illustrations of black participation during the Civil War were not uncommon.

This non-regulation identification disk was sold by the camp or regimental sutler. It belonged to 18-year-old Edward Staples, a barber, who was born in Richmond, Virginia. He joined Company L, 5th Regiment Massachusetts Colored Cavalry on April 15, 1864. This regiment was a state volunteer unit and not a federal regiment. It was not one of the regiments in the United States Colored Troops.
Recto: George Washington born February 22, 1732
Verso: Edward Staples, Co. L 5th Mass. Cav Richmond Va.
Material: Brass

Memorial placard of Company B, 10th Regiment, U.S. Artillery (Heavy), United States Colored Troops. This regiment was originally the 1st Regiment Louisiana Heavy Artillery (African Descent) until redesignated 1st Corps d'Afrique Heavy Artillery and later redesignated the 10th Regiment, U.S. Artillery (Heavy), U.S. Colored Troops.

Artillery Soldiers

First Sergeant A Company, wearing frock coat with sergeant's stripes on sleeve and non-commissioned officer's brass shoulder scales. He is holding the Model 1840 Artillery sword in his hand. This sixth plate ambrotype is 2 3/4 by 3 1/4 inches.

An artillery private is wearing a shell jacket with red piping in this is a one-eighth plate tintype. A tintype is made in the same process as an ambrotype but the sticky, wet emulsion is on lightweight metal instead of glass.

Elmira Prison Camp, Elmira, New York

According to Clay Holmes in his *The Elmira Prison Camp*, "At barracks No. 1, there were 200 colored drafted men and substitutes, organized into two companies, armed and equipped, doing Guard Duty. Thirty of these men are detailed as a Patrol Guard inside the enclosure at Prisoners Camp." Guarding Confederate Prisoners was not an uncommon detail for many regiments of the U.S. Colored Troops.

A Northern sarcastic form of expression on the imprisonment of Jefferson Davis in *carte de visite* format. Fort Monroe, a stone and brick fortress near Newport News, Virginia, was where General Ben Butler coined the phrase "contraband of war." The fort served as headquarters for the Army of the James.

On May 11, 1865, Davis was captured; two days later he was placed in Fort Monroe. He was imprisoned there for two years until his friends had him released on bail. Armed sentries were posted inside and outside his cell twenty-four hours a day with orders not to converse with him.

Reminders of the loved ones at home were most important to the soldier away for the first time. *Cartes de visite* in a small photo holder were most cherished by the troops, who would carry the photos in their haversacks.

A small cased tintype (1/16 plate) could be found in the soldier's haversack if he were fortunate enough to have such an image. These would have belonged to the soldier from the North, for the soldier from the South was most often a former slave and did not have such personal belongings as part of his lifestyle.

The colored man among the group of soldiers in front of the woodchopper's hut, Brandy Station, is probably a cook for the group. Contrabands found employment around camp. They knew where to acquire supplies and knew the people and the area, an asset to an organization in the field.

Not all colored men wearing Civil War uniforms were soldiers. It is more obvious when one sees men in parts of uniforms but it is sometimes questionable when one is fully uniformed. The regulation called for men being employed by the government in certain capacities would receive one ration a day plus clothing. The clothing the government would issue would be army clothing, hence the confusion. A photograph of a colored man in parts of a uniform or in a uniform appearing disarranged is a way of detecting this type of individual. When a soldier in the U.S. Colored Troops had his picture taken, he appeared neatly dressed and in a pose of pride.

Civilians in Uniform

The man in vest and frock coat is Gilbert Montgomery, sub-cook in the 4th U.S. Colored Cavalry.

"Rebel Pickets"

REBEL NEGRO PICKETS AS SEEN THROUGH A FIELD-GLASS.

To offset the balance of the supposed wickedness of using Negroes on the Northern side, the artist Theodore R. Davis sent this sketch of colored rebel pickets being used at Fredericksburg as seen through the field glasses of a Union officer and told to Davis. This appeared on the front page of *Harpers Weekly*, January 10, 1863.

Showing the Confederates using fully armed slaves on picket duty was to help those proponents of the North in using soldiers of any color to help fight against the insurgents.

It was not until March 13, 1865, that President Jefferson Davis signed a "Negro Soldier Law" which authorized the enlistment of slaves as soldiers. A few companies of colored soldiers were enrolled in Richmond and elsewhere. The war was over before anything could come of it.

Medals, Weapons, Flags & Battles

Medal of Honor Recipients, U.S. Colored Soldiers

Enlisted Men	*Rank*	*Regiment*	*Date of Issue*
1. Barnes, William H.	Private	38th	April 6, 1865
2. Beaty, Powhatan	Private	5th	April 6, 1865
3. Bronson, James H.	1st Sgt.	5th	April 6, 1865
4. Carney, William H.	Sergeant	54th Mass.	May 23, 1900
5. Dorsey, Decautur	Sergeant	39th	Nov. 8, 1865
6. Fleetwood, Christian	Sgt. Major	4th	April 6, 1865
7. Gardiner, James	Private	36th	April 6, 1865
8. Harris, James H.	Sergeant	38th	Feb. 18, 1874
9. Hawkins, Thomas	Sgt. Major	6th	Feb. 8, 1870
10. Hilton, Alfred B.	Sergeant	4th	April 6, 1865
11. Holland, Milton M.	Sgt. Major	5th	April 6, 1865
12. James, Miles	Corporal	36th	April 6, 1865
13. Kelley, Alexander	1st Sgt.	6th	April 6, 1865
14. Pinn, Robert	1st Sgt.	5th	April 6, 1865
15. Ratcliff, Edward	1st Sgt.	38th	April 6, 1865
16. Veal, Charles	Private	4th	April 6, 1865

"The old flag never touched the ground, boys."

SERGT. WILLIAM H. CARNEY, of Co. C.

WITH THE FLAG HE SAVED AT WAGNER.

Sergeant William H. Carney, Company C, 54th Massachusetts, received the Medal of Honor on May 23, 1900, for his participation in the Battle of Fort Wagner. Although his deed was the first for a colored soldier (July 18, 1863), he was the last of the colored Civil War soldiers to receive the medal. His citation reads: When the color sergeant was shot down, this soldier grasped the flag, led the way to the parapet, and planted the colors thereon. When the troops fell back he brought off the flag, under a fierce fire in which he was twice severely wounded." He took pride in the fact that the flag never touched the ground." Carney also received the Gillmore Medal.

Sergeant Major Christian Fleetwood of the 4th U.S. Colored Troops is wearing the uniform of a major, 7th Infantry Regiment, Washington, D.C., National Guard. On his chest, from the left, are an Army of the James Medal, a Medal of Honor, and what appears to be a National Guard Medal. There was no regulation at this time for the placement of medals on the uniform. Fleetwood received the Medal of Honor for his participation in the Battle of Chapin's Farm on September 29 and 30, 1864. The citation reads: Seized the colors, after two color bearers had been shot down and bore them nobly through the fight." The main reason for awarding the Medal of Honor during this period of history was the capturing of the enemy flag or protecting your own flag.

The Gillmore Medal was authorized October 28, 1863. Considered a Medal of Honor for Gallant and Meritorious conduct during the operations before Charleston, S.C. Only three percent of the men that have been in action or on duty in the batteries or trenches could be awarded this medal. General Quincy A. Gillmore had 400 bronze medals struck. A number of soldiers in the U.S. Colored Troops were recipients of this prestigious medal. William H. Carney of the 54th Massachusetts Infantry Regiment (Colored), a Medal of Honor winner, has been photographed wearing the Gillmore Medal. At this time a detailed list of colored recipients is not known.

The Army of the James Medal, commonly called the Butler Medal, is the only medal ever struck for colored troops. General Benjamin Butler himself designed and paid for these medals after the Battle of Chapin's Farm. Only 197 silver medals were struck. The medal is inscribed on the verso side when translated, "Liberty came to them by the sword U.S. Colored Troops." Inscribed on the recto side is "Distinguished for Courage, Campaign before Richmond 1864." The medal had a red, white and blue ribbon with a wreath embossed "Army of the James."

The Civil War Campaign Medal was authorized by the War Department in 1907 for military service from April 15, 1861, to April 9, 1865—or for service in Texas to August 20, 1866. This included men of the U.S. Colored Troops. The original ribbon had a narrow white stripe in the center, flanked on either side by equal stripes of red, white and blue. This was changed in 1913 to half blue, on the left, and half gray.

U.S. Colored Troops were issued the best weapons available to fulfill their perceived mission. Black and white soldiers were given the same arms to fight for their country.

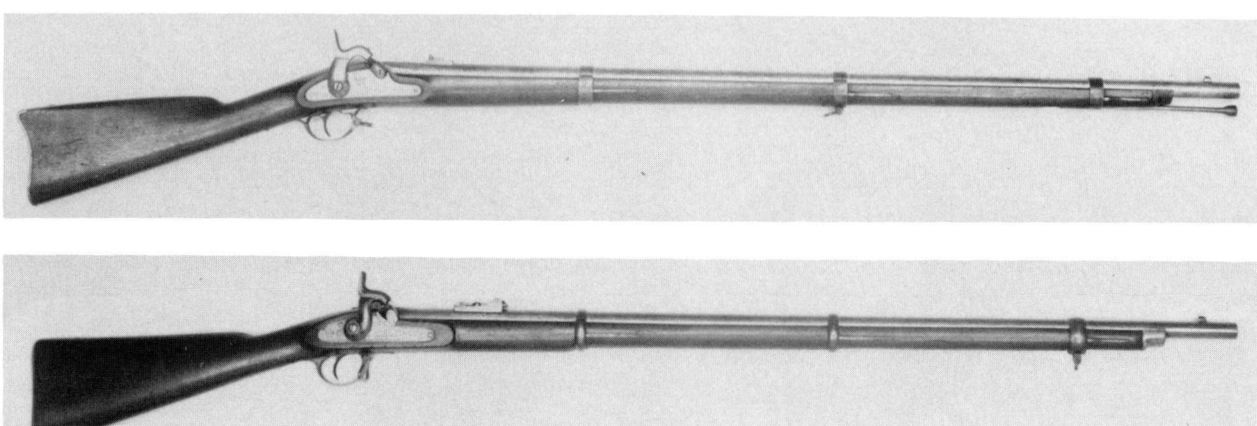

Front-line combat units were issued first-class weapons: M1861 Springfield rifled musket, .58 cal. (top) and P1853 Enfield rifled musket, .577 cal. (bottom) imported from England.

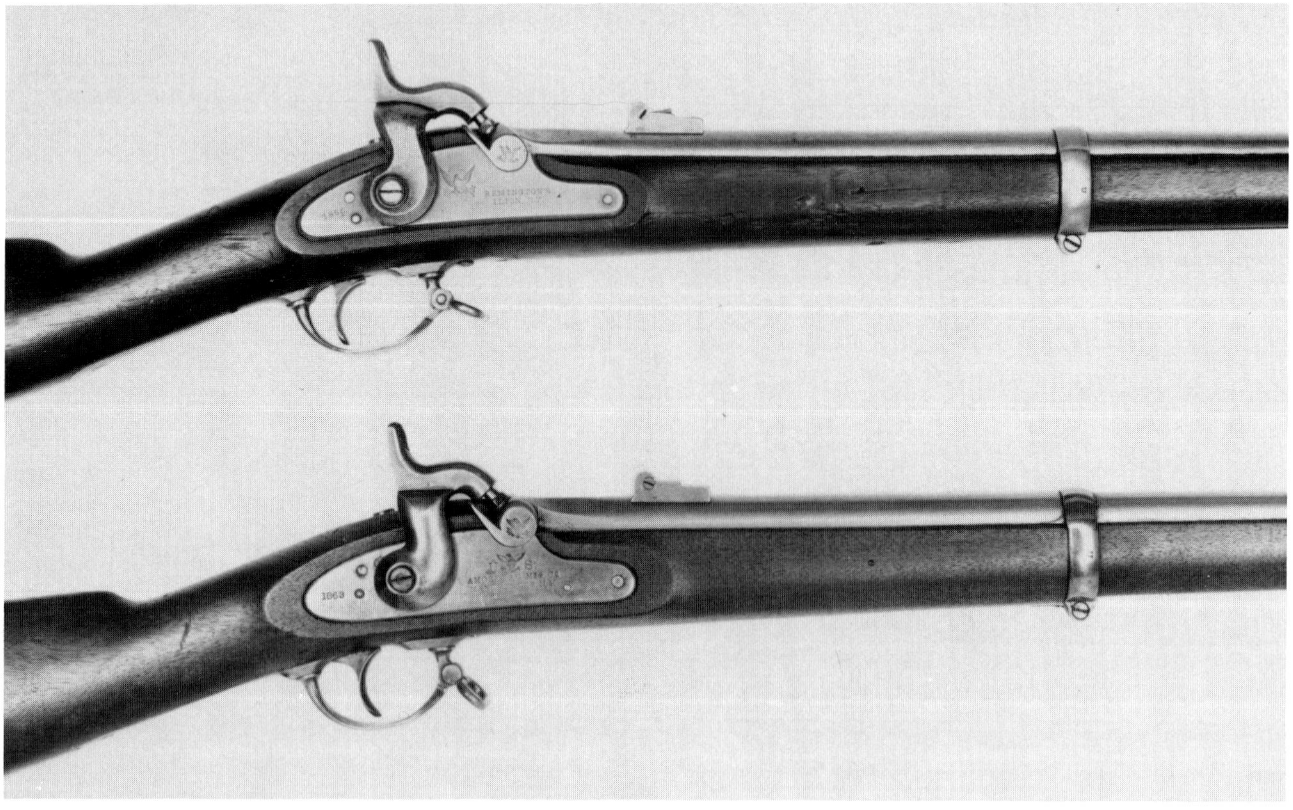

Other first-class weapons were: U.S. M1863 rifled musket, .58 cal. (top) and U.S. M1861 Special Model rifled musket, .58 cal. (bottom).

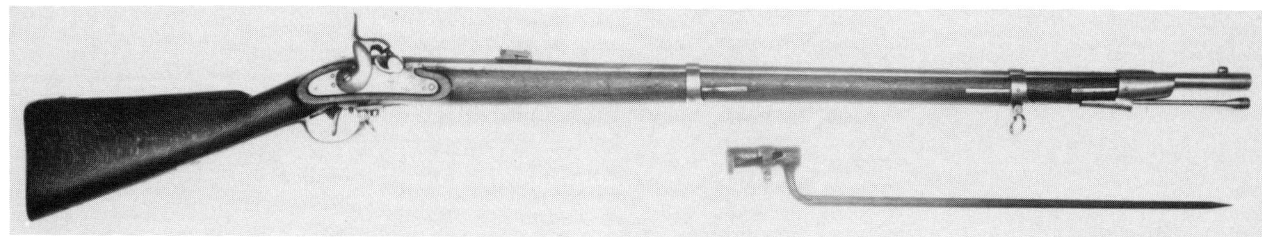

One example of a second-class arm is the M1855 Austrian "Lorenz" rifled musket, .54 cal., shown here with its bayonet.

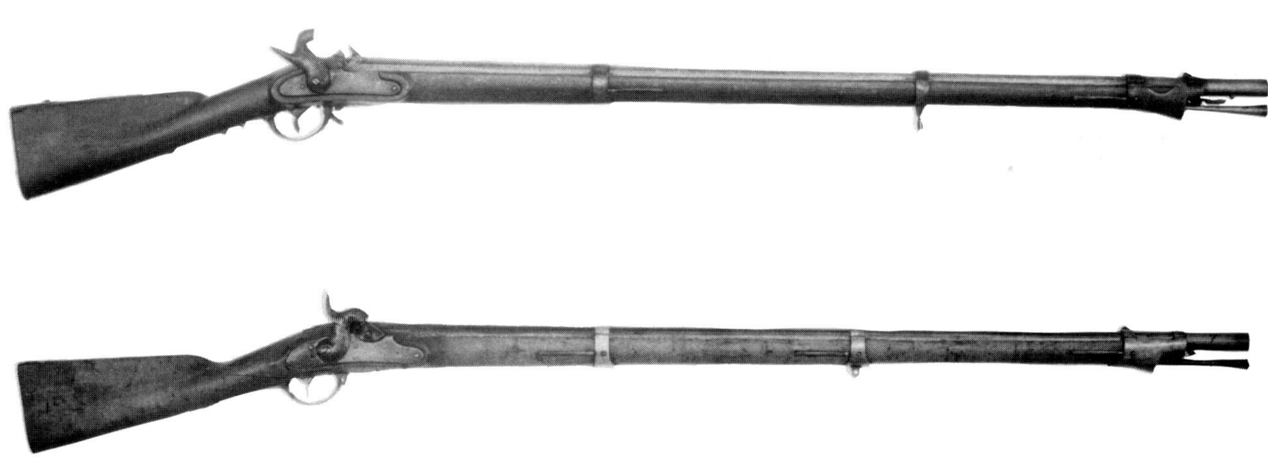

Third-class guns were usually issued to garrison troops, and included: Austrian rifled musket, .69 cal. (top) and Prussian musket, .69 cal. (bottom).

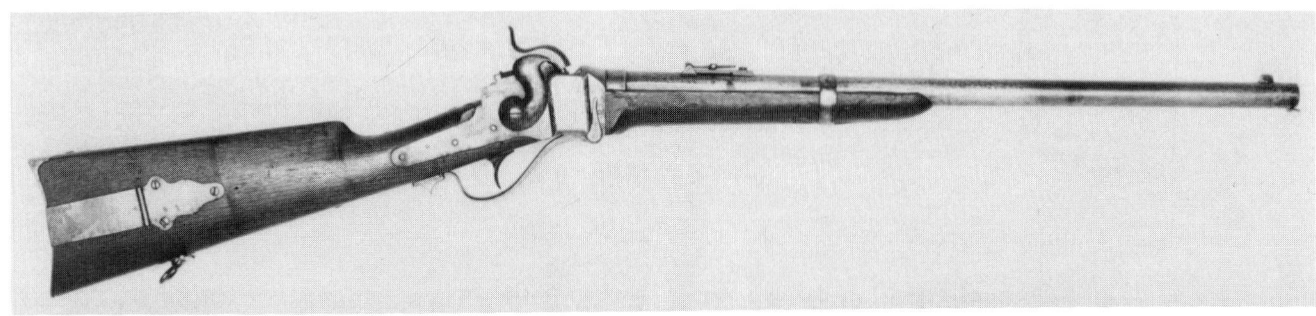

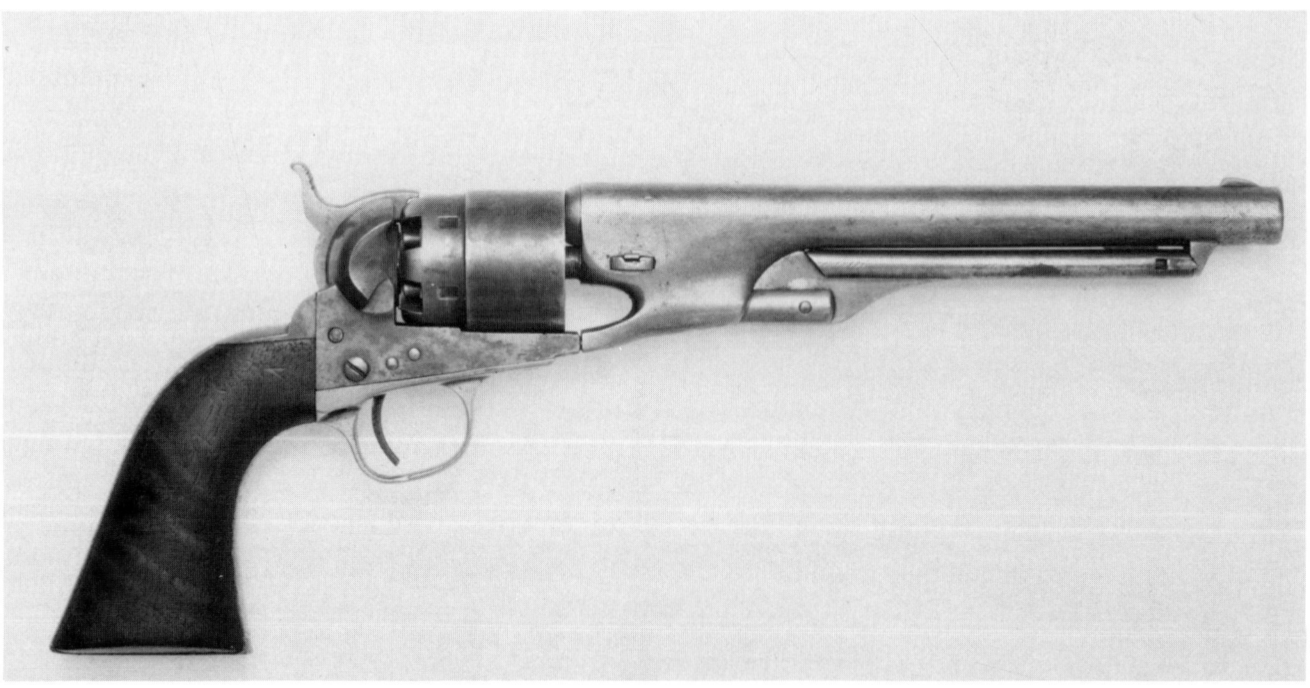

Among the many types of cavalry weapons were the .52 cal. Sharps M1859 breechloading carbine (top) and the .44 cal. Colt M1860 "Army Holster" revolver (bottom).

Regimental Flags

Color sergeant of the 108th Regiment U.S. Colored Troops, with regimental standard. Each infantry regiment had a blue silk flag similar to the one shown. This is a regulation flag.

A non-regulation regimental flag of the 24th U.S. Colored Troops attributed to David Bustill Bowser. Its motto, "Let Soldiers in War be Citizens in Peace" is most significant in the spirit of Frederick Douglass. The flag was presented by the citizens of Philadelphia.

Obverse (left) and reverse (right) of the regimental color of the 6th U.S. Colored Troops. The artwork on this flag is also attributed to David Bustill Bowser of Philadelphia and has the motto "Freedom for All" on the obverse. This flag was rescued by Sergeant Major Thomas R. Hawkins during the assault at New Market Heights, Virginia, on September 29, 1864. Five years after the end of the war, Hawkins received the Medal of Honor for his valor.

This is the national color of the 37th Regiment, U.S. Colored Troops, 1st Brigade, 3rd Division, 25th Army Corps.

The 37th Regiment was organized at Norfolk, Virginia, from January 30 to September 19, 1864, as the 3rd Regiment North Carolina Volunteer Infantry (African Descent), to serve three years. Its designation was changed to 37th Regiment U.S.C.T. on February 8, 1864. It was mustered out of service February 11, 1867.

General Butler had ordered the 37th U.S. Colored Troops to have the words "New Market Heights" inscribed upon their colors for their gallantry in carrying the enemy's works at that point on September 29, 1864. The quartermaster was directed to furnish a new standard of colors to this regiment with the inscription ordered. The flag was supplied, but contained an error—they were part of the 18th Army Corps and not the 24th Army Corps. The flag was probably never issued.

25th Army Corps veteran's badge of Private Alfred Willis, Co. D, 45th U.S.C.T. Willis was mustered into service on July 1, 1864, and mustered out with his company on November 4, 1865.

Honorable Discharge badge issued by the state of West Virginia and inscribed on the rim "Alexander Wade, Co. G, 45th U.S.C.T." Wade was mustered into service on July 29, 1864, and participated with his regiment in Abraham Lincoln's second inauguration procession in March 1865.

Reunion badge of a member of Company G, 5th U.S. Colored Troops, redesignated from the 127th Ohio Regiment Volunteer Infantry (Colored).

All black soldiers from the State Volunteers, Corps d'Afrique, or the U.S. Colored Troops were entitled to the Grand Army of the Republic Medal.

This Grand Army of the Republic veteran from Massachusetts still sits a horse in a military fashion. He may have been in the 5th Massachusetts Cavalry. He has a GAR wreath on his hat. Notice the two reunion ribbons on his coat.

The Fort Pillow massacre of colored soldiers on April 12, 1864, devastated Battery F, 2nd Light Artillery, and the 11th (new) U.S. Colored Troops. An investigation by the U.S. Congress' Committee on the Conduct of the War followed. After this massacre, colored troops had "Remember Fort Pillow" as their battle cry. The Confederate forces were part of Major General Nathan Bedford Forrest's command.

Major General Nathan Bedford Forrest enlisted as a private in the 7th Tennessee Cavalry, C.S.A. and rose to the rank of Lieutenant General.

Three colored regiments participated in the Battle of Olustee, Florida, on February 20, 1864. They were the 8th and 35th U.S. Colored Troops and the 54th Massachusetts Infantry Regiment (Colored). Those colored soldiers captured by the Confederates were sent to Andersonville.

The two-day Battle of Nashville, Tennessee, on December 15 and 16, 1864, involved Battery A, 2nd Light Artillery and the 12th, 13th, 14th, 17th, 18th, and 100th Infantry Regiments of the U.S. Colored Troops. This was part of the Franklin and Nashville Campaign. Six officers and 80 enlisted men were killed; fourteen officers and 309 enlisted men were wounded. The 18th regiment had the heaviest losses.

Documents

U. S. INFANTRY TACTICS,

FOR THE

INSTRUCTION, EXERCISE, AND MANŒUVRES,

OF

THE SOLDIER, A COMPANY, LINE OF SKIRMISHERS, AND BATTALION;

FOR THE USE OF

THE COLORED TROOPS

OF THE

UNITED STATES INFANTRY.

PREPARED UNDER DIRECTION OF THE WAR DEPARTMENT.

NEW YORK:
D. VAN NOSTRAND, 192 BROADWAY.
1863.

WAR DEPARTMENT,
Washington, March 9, 1863.

This system of United States Infantry Tactics, prepared under the direction of the War Department for the use of the colored troops of the United States Infantry, having been approved by the President, is adopted for the instruction of such troops.

EDWIN M. STANTON,
Secretary of War.

This manual of infantry tactics for the colored troops was approved two months before the formation of the Bureau of Colored Troops. For all practical purposes, it is the same as the three-volume set by Silas Casey on infantry tactics for the white troops, but it is in one volume.

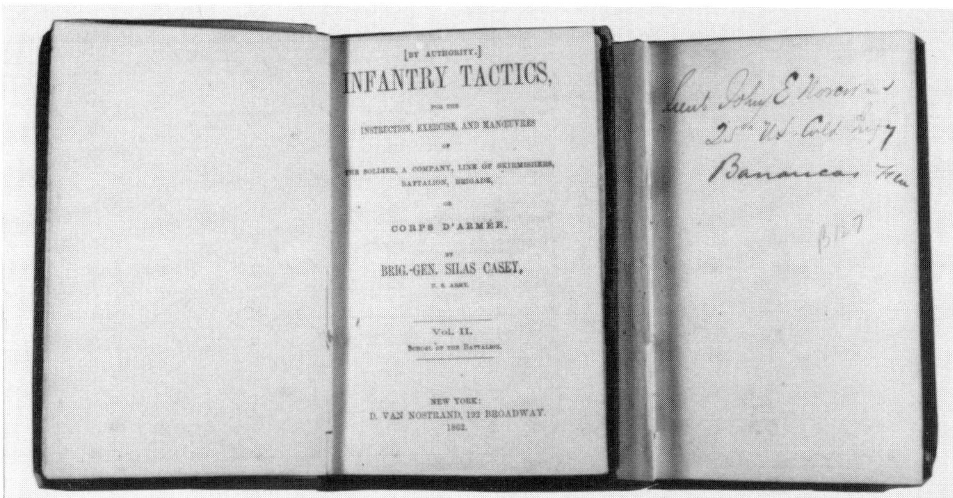

This volume two of a three- volume set of Casey's *Infantry Tactics* belonged to Lieutenant John E. Norcross, 25th U.S. Colored Infantry. For all practical purposes this is the same book as *Infantry Tactics for Colored Troops*. Many officers who had prior experience would probably have used their Casey's *Infantry Tactics* instead of acquiring a new one for colored troops.

Second Lieutenant John E. Norcross, brevet captain, June 20, 1865, Company G, 25th U.S. Colored Troops, enlisted at Camp William Penn and had a relatively easy tour of duty. He enlisted for three years, mustering into service April 26, 1864, and mustering out June 20, 1865. He had duty in the defenses of New Orleans and the regiment was garrisoned for six months at Fort Barrancas, Florida, as noted in his manuals.

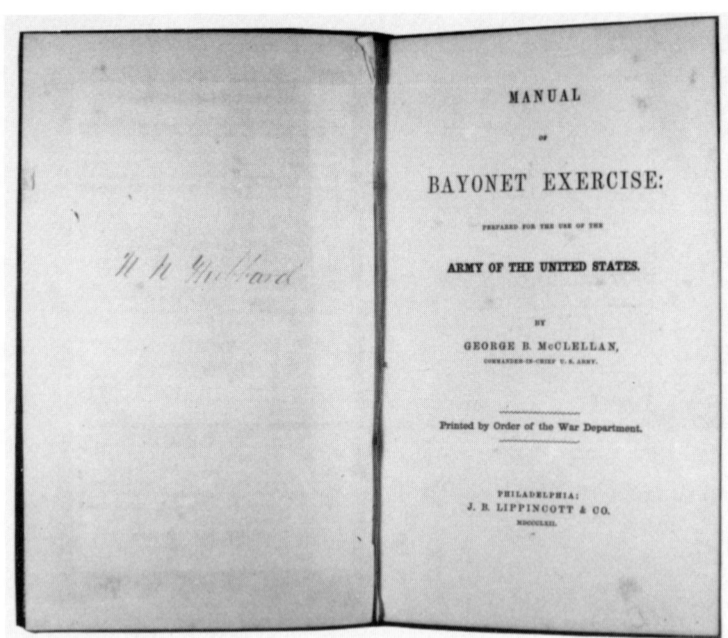

N N Hubbard

MANUAL

OF

BAYONET EXERCISE:

PREPARED FOR THE USE OF THE

ARMY OF THE UNITED STATES.

BY

GEORGE B. McCLELLAN,

COMMANDER-IN-CHIEF U. S. ARMY.

Printed by Order of the War Department.

PHILADELPHIA:
J. B. LIPPINCOTT & CO.
MDCCCLXII.

Company "B"
6th Regt U S Colred Troop

This *Manual of Bayonet Exercise* by George B. McClellan belonged to First Lieutenant Nathaniel N. Hubbard, Company B, 6th Regiment, U.S. Colored Troops. Hubbard was wounded at New Market Heights, Virginia, September 29, 1864. He was discharged on a surgeon's certificate, March 3, 1865.

Officers who did not have much experience leading men would use the manuals to help them with their "on the job training." The 6th Regiment, U.S. Colored Troops, was one of the William Penn regiments. The 6th Regiment had a distinguished military record, fighting in Virginia at Williamsburg, Petersburg, Chapin's Farm, and Sugar Loaf Hill.

Head Quarters, U. S. Forces,

HILTON HEAD, FORT PULASKI, ST. HELENA AND TYBEE ISLANDS.

Hilton Head, S. C., Oct. 5 1864.

Countersign: Rappahannock

By order of GEORGE W. BAIRD,

COLONEL 32d U. S. C. T.,

Commanding District.

W. C. MANNING,

CAPT. & ACT. ASS'T ADJ'T GENERAL.

OFFICIAL: W. Pollak

Lieut. & A. A. D. C.

The countersign or "watchword" is issued daily. Usually the countersign is the name of a battle. It was given to such persons entitled to pass during the night and to officers, non-commissioned officers, and sentinels of the guard.

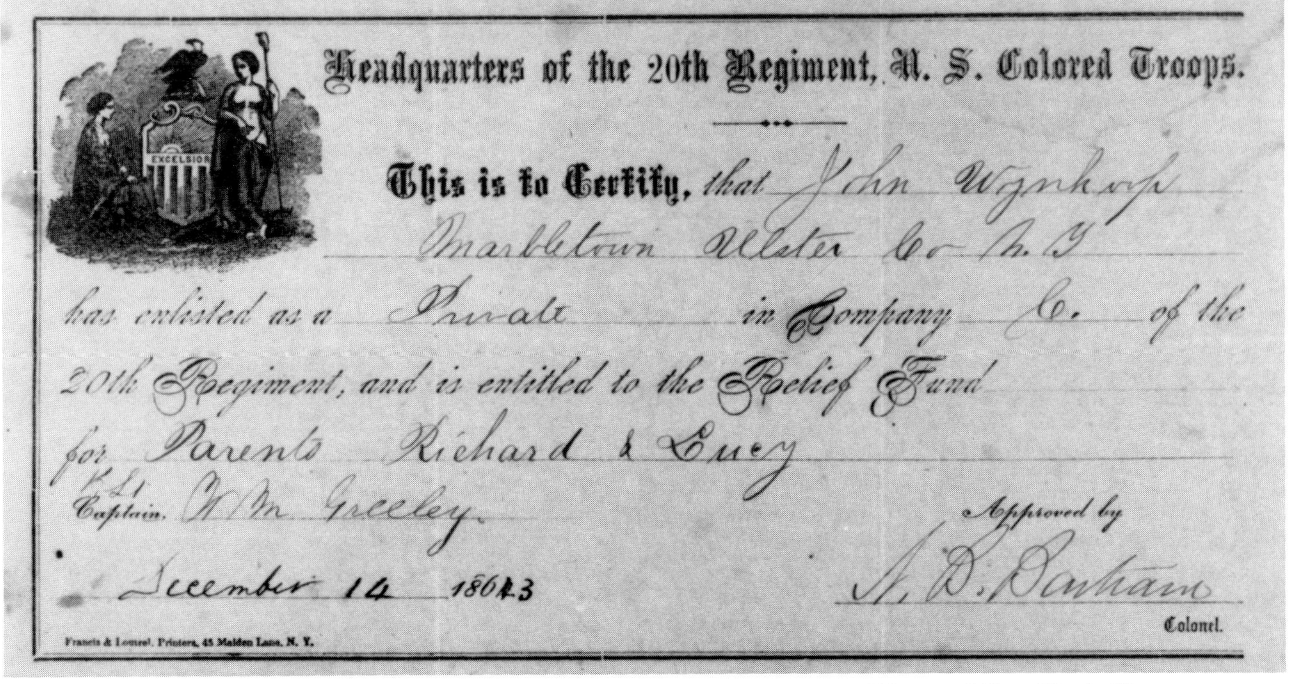

Headquarters of the 20th Regiment, U. S. Colored Troops.

This is to Certify, that John Wynkoop Marbletown Ulster Co N. Y has enlisted as a Private in Company C. of the 20th Regiment, and is entitled to the Relief Fund for Parents Richard & Lucy

Capt. Wm Greeley, Captain.

December 14 1864 3

Approved by N. B. Bartram, Colonel.

Francis & Loutrel, Printers, 45 Maiden Lane, N. Y.

The 20th U.S. Colored Troops was organized on Rikers Island, in the East River, of New York City.

The parents of Private John Wynhos are entitled to the Regimental Relief Funds.

The 20th U.S. Colored Troops was one of the three regiments formed in New York state. They marched down Broadway to the cheers of New Yorkers eight months after black people were killed on the streets, men hanged from lampposts, and a Children Orphans Asylum burned.

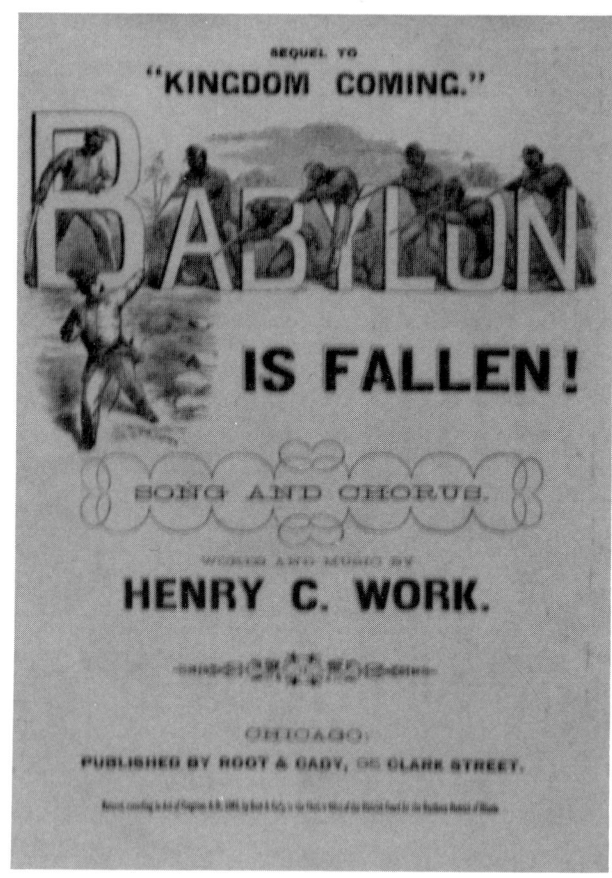

At the beginning, the Civil War colored soldiers were depicted in a comical fashion. After the battles of Port Hudson, Fort Wagner, Chapin's Farm, the Crater and Petersburg, the question of the fighting capabilities of the black soldier was not longer in doubt. They fought well and earned the respect of their comrades-in-arms. As the war progressed, they were shown as respected fighting men of the U.S. Army.

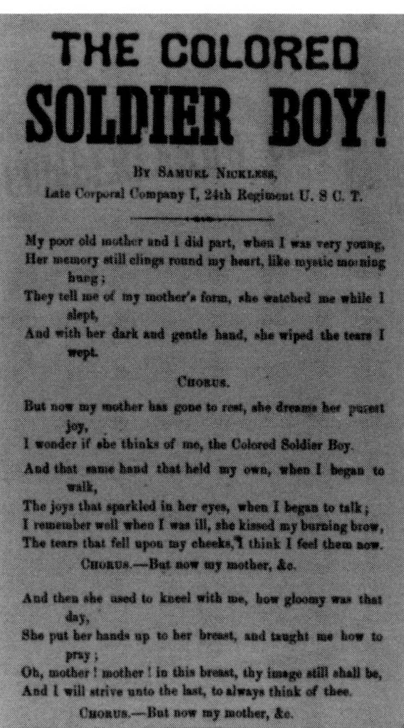

THE COLORED
SOLDIER BOY!

By Samuel Nickless,
Late Corporal Company I, 24th Regiment U. S C. T.

My poor old mother and I did part, when I was very young,
Her memory still clings round my heart, like mystic morning hung;
They tell me of my mother's form, she watched me while I slept,
And with her dark and gentle hand, she wiped the tears I wept.

Chorus.

But now my mother has gone to rest, she dreams her purest joy,
I wonder if she thinks of me, the Colored Soldier Boy.

And that same hand that held my own, when I began to walk,
The joys that sparkled in her eyes, when I began to talk;
I remember well when I was ill, she kissed my burning brow,
The tears that fell upon my cheeks, I think I feel them now.
Chorus.—But now my mother, &c.

And then she used to kneel with me, how gloomy was that day,
She put her hands up to her breast, and taught me how to pray;
Oh, mother! mother! in this breast, thy image still shall be,
And I will strive unto the last, to always think of thee.
Chorus.—But now my mother, &c.

JOHNSON'S
CARD & JOB PRINTING OFFICE,
No. 7 North Tenth St., Phila.

Along with the patriotic themes and propaganda, a number of items were printed depicting the colored soldier. "The Colored Soldier Boy" was a poem written by Corporal Samuel Nickless of Company I, 24th Regiment U.S. Colored Troops. Nickless also wrote a variation to this poem. He had entered the service March 21, 1865, for one year and was sick at the time of muster out October 1, 1865. The 24th Regiment was the last regiment to be at Camp William Penn. It was sent to Washington, D.C., and duty at Camp Casey. The 24th also had duty at Point Lookout, Maryland, guarding prisoners. From there it went to Roanoke headquarters, then Richmond, Virginia, and mustered out.

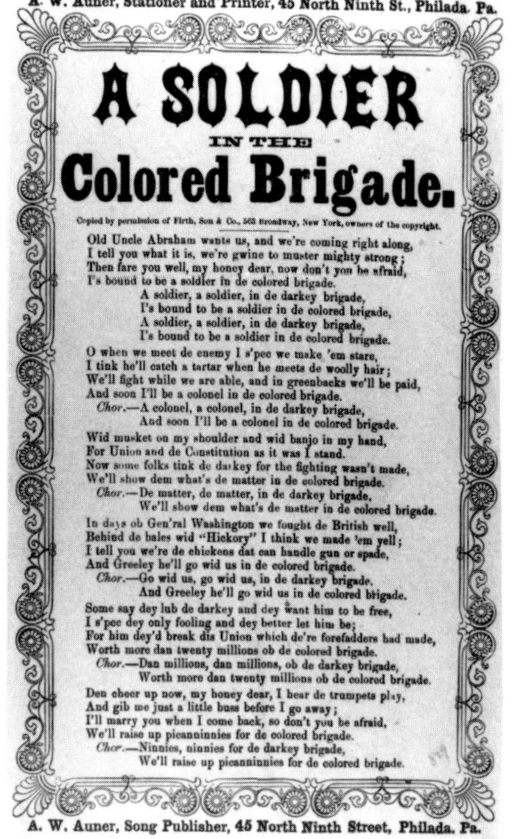

A. W. Auner, Stationer and Printer, 45 North Ninth St., Philada. Pa.

A SOLDIER
IN THE
Colored Brigade.

Copied by permission of Firth, Son & Co., 563 Broadway, New York, owners of the copyright.

Old Uncle Abraham wants us, and we're coming right along,
I tell you what it is, we're gwine to muster mighty strong;
Then fare you well, my honey dear, now don't you be afraid,
I's bound to be a soldier in de colored brigade.
A soldier, a soldier, in de darkey brigade,
I's bound to be a soldier in de colored brigade,
A soldier, a soldier, in de darkey brigade,
I's bound to be a soldier in de colored brigade.

O when we meet de enemy I s'pec we make 'em stare,
I tink he'll catch a tartar when he meets de woolly hair;
We'll fight while we are able, and in greenbacks we'll be paid,
And soon I'll be a colonel in de colored brigade.
Chor.—A colonel, a colonel, in de darkey brigade,
And soon I'll be a colonel in de colored brigade.

Wid musket on my shoulder and wid banjo in my hand,
For Union and de Constitution as it was I stand.
Now some folks tink de darkey for the fighting wasn't made,
We'll show dem what's de matter in de colored brigade.
Chor.—De matter, de matter, in de darkey brigade,
We'll show dem what's de matter in de colored brigade.

In days ob Gen'ral Washington we fought de British well,
Behind de bales wid "Hickory" I think we made 'em yell;
I tell you we're de chickens dat can handle gun or spade,
And Greeley he'll go wid us in de colored brigade.
Chor.—Go wid us, go wid us, in de darkey brigade.
And Greeley he'll go wid us in de colored brigade.

Some say dey lub de darkey and dey want him to be free,
I s'pec dey only fooling and dey better let him be;
For him dey'd break dis Union which de're forefadders had made,
Worth more dan twenty millions ob de colored brigade.
Chor.—Dan millions, dan millions, ob de darkey brigade,
Worth more dan twenty millions ob de colored brigade.

Den cheer up now, my honey dear, I hear de trumpets play,
And gib me just a little buss before I go away;
I'll marry you when I come back, so don't you be afraid,
We'll raise up picanninnies for de colored brigade.
Chor.—Ninnies, ninnies for de darkey brigade,
We'll raise up picanninnies for de colored brigade.

A. W. Auner, Song Publisher, 45 North Ninth Street, Philada. Pa.

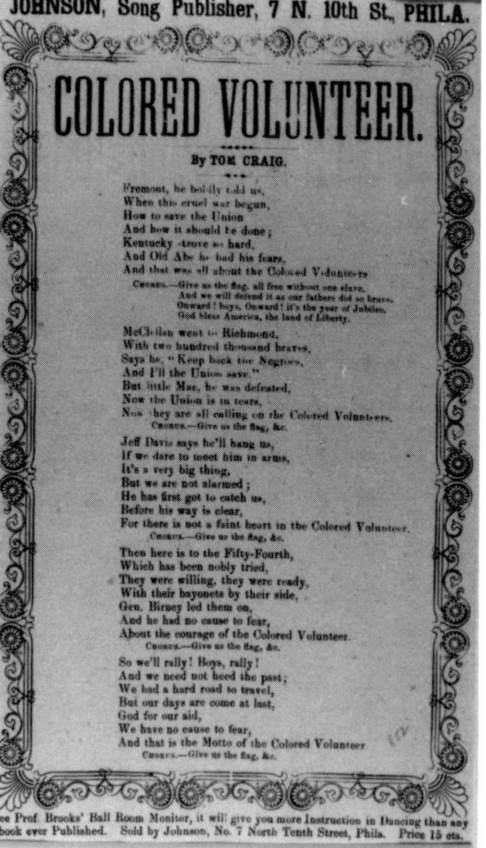

JOHNSON, Song Publisher, 7 N. 10th St., PHILA.

COLORED VOLUNTEER.

By TOM CRAIG.

Fremont, he boldly told us,
When this cruel war begun,
How to save the Union
And how it should be done;
Kentucky strove so hard,
And Old Abe he had his fears,
And that was all about the Colored Volunteers
Chorus.—Give us the flag, all free without one slave,
And we will defend it as our fathers did so brave.
Onward! boys, Onward! it's the year of Jubilee,
God bless America, the land of Liberty.

McClellan went to Richmond,
With two hundred thousand braves,
Says he, "Keep back the Negroes,
And I'll the Union save."
But little Mac, he was defeated,
Now the Union is in tears,
Now they are all calling on the Colored Volunteers.
Chorus.—Give us the flag, &c.

Jeff Davis says he'll hang us,
If we dare to meet him in arms,
It's a very big thing,
But we are not alarmed;
He has first got to catch us,
Before his way is clear,
For there is not a faint heart in the Colored Volunteer.
Chorus.—Give us the flag, &c.

Then here is to the Fifty-Fourth,
Which has been nobly tried,
They were willing, they were ready,
With their bayonets by their side,
Gen. Birney led them on,
And he had no cause to fear,
About the courage of the Colored Volunteer.
Chorus.—Give us the flag, &c.

So we'll rally! Boys, rally!
And we need not heed the past;
We had a hard road to travel,
But our days are come at last,
God for our aid,
We have no cause to fear,
And that is the Motto of the Colored Volunteer
Chorus.—Give us the flag, &c.

See Prof. Brooks' Ball Room Monitor, it will give you more Instruction in Dancing than any book ever Published. Sold by Johnson, No. 7 North Tenth Street, Phila. Price 15 cts.

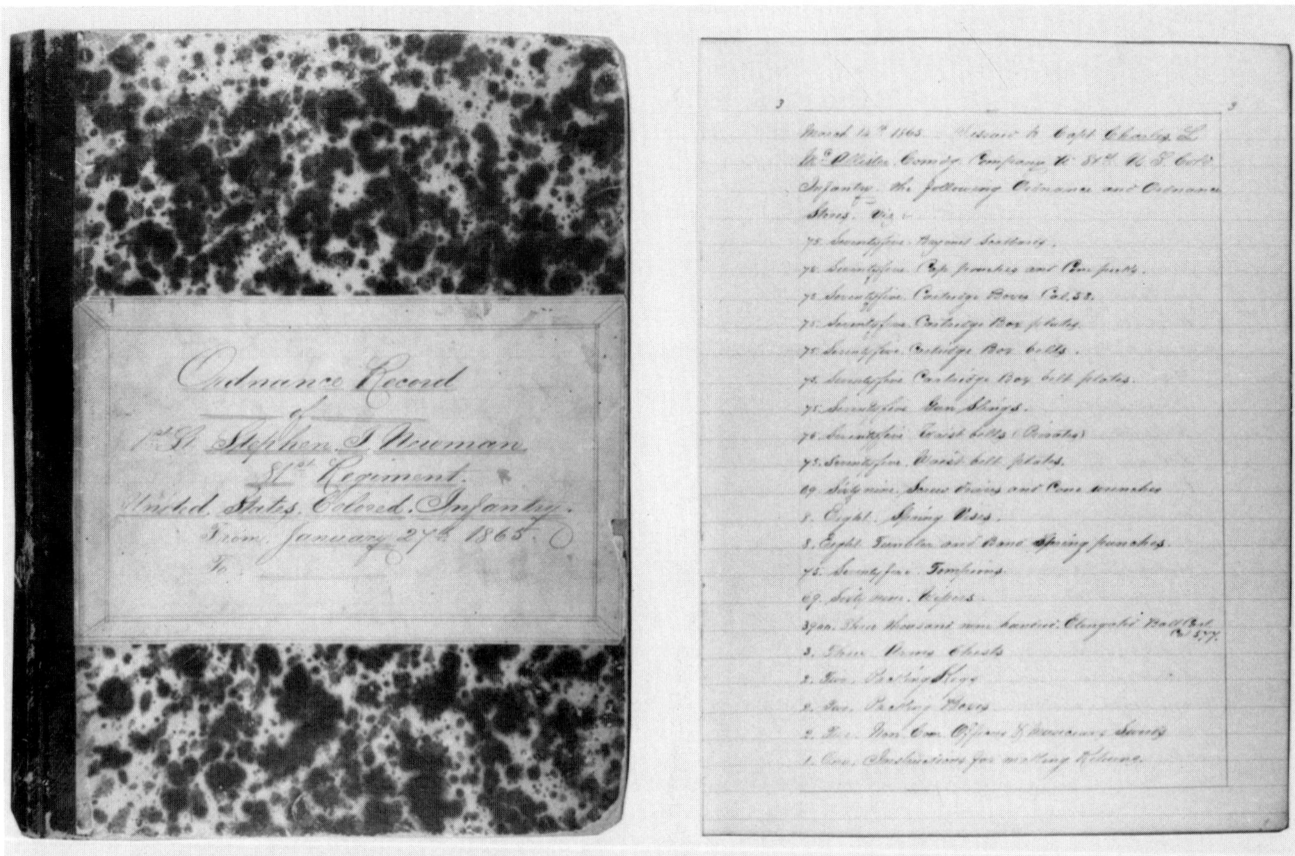

Ordnance Record Book of First Lieutenant James I. Newman of the 81st Infantry Regiment, U.S. Colored Troops. The 81st was originally formed as the 9th Regiment Infantry, Corps d'Afrique, and later redesignated. It was organized at Port Hudson, Louisiana, to serve three years. Record books such as this attest that colored troops were not issued inferior weapons because they were Negroes.

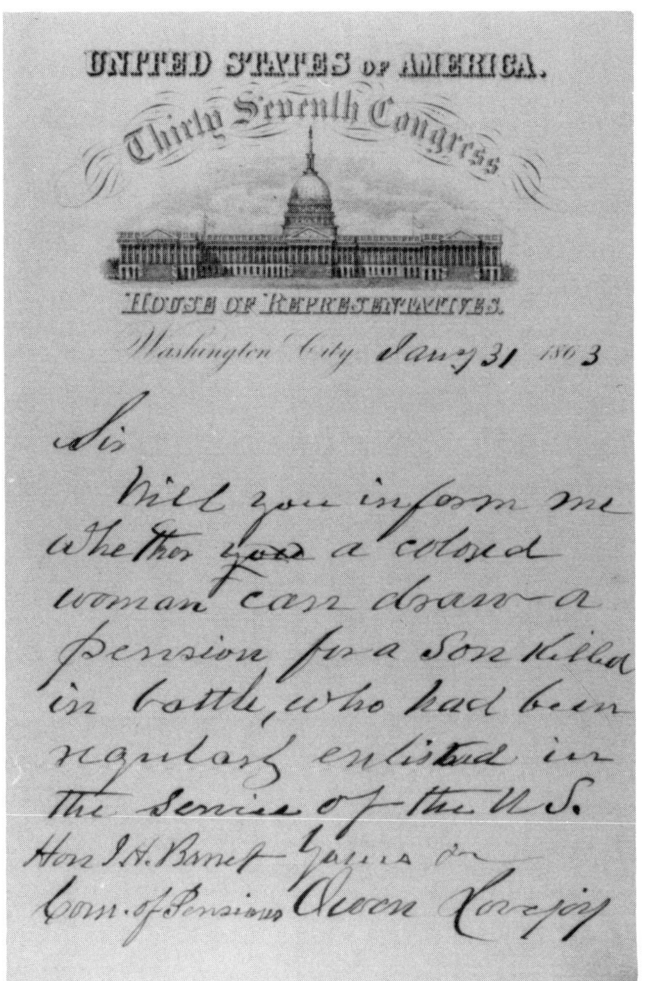

UNITED STATES of AMERICA.

Thirty Seventh Congress

HOUSE OF REPRESENTATIVES.

Washington City Jany 31 1863

Sir

Will you inform me whether ~~you~~ a colored woman can draw a pension for a son killed in battle, who had been regularly enlisted in the Service of the U.S.

Hon J. H. Barret Yours &c

Com. of Pensions Owen Lovejoy

This letter by Owen Lovejoy from the House of Representatives to the Commissioner of Pensions on January 31, 1863, proposes an interesting question pertaining to colored troops before the Bureau of Colored Troops was formed. Lovejoy wrote asking "whether a colored woman can draw a pension for a son killed in battle, who had been regularly enlisted in the Service of the U.S." If the question is about someone who has been killed, it must mean one of the five regiments formed prior to the Emancipation Proclamation.

State of Maryland,

Adjutant General's Office,

Annapolis, May 7th 1866

I hereby certify that from the Records of this Office it appears that Joseph Pullitt of Co. "G", 9th Regiment U.S.C.T. ~~Maryland~~ Volunteers, Was "Killed in action

Duplicate

Jno. S. Berry

Brig. Gen'l and Adj't Gen'l.

After the war there was much paperwork by the Adjutant General's Office of the many states in which colored soldiers claimed as their origin. This paperwork is being processed by a widow for a soldier of the 9th Infantry Regiment U.S. Colored Troops who was "killed in action." This request was made before the regiment had been mustered out of service on November 26, 1866.

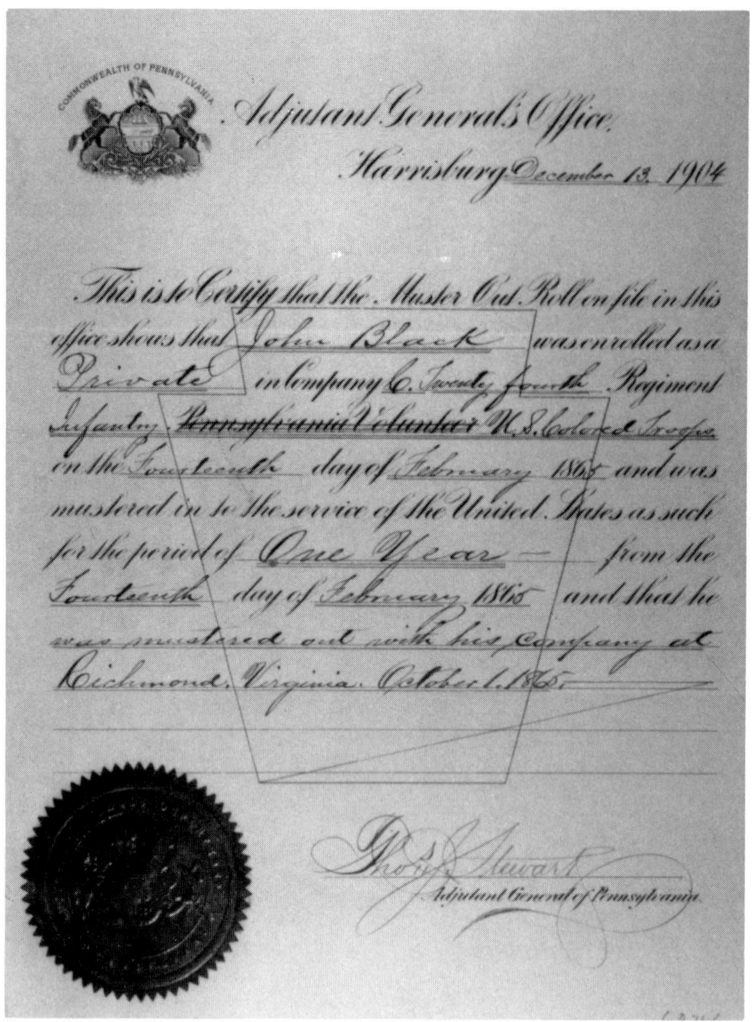

COMMONWEALTH OF PENNSYLVANIA

Adjutant General's Office.

Harrisburg, December 13, 1904

This is to Certify that the Muster Out Roll on file in this office shows that John Black was enrolled as a Private in Company C. Twenty fourth Regiment Infantry ~~Pennsylvania Volunteer~~ U.S. Colored Troops on the Fourteenth day of February 1865 and was mustered in to the service of the United States as such for the period of One Year — from the Fourteenth day of February 1865 and that he was mustered out with his company at Richmond, Virginia. October 1. 1865.

Thos. J. Stewart

Adjutant General of Pennsylvania.

This is a statement from the Adjutant General's Office, Harrisburg, Pennsylvania, dated December 13, 1904, to the effect that John Black was a private in the 24th U.S. Colored Troops. Notice that "Pennsylvania volunteer" was crossed out because the U.S. Colored Troops were not part of Pennsylvania forces. Black enlisted for one year from February 14, 1865, and was discharged October 1, 1865, at Richmond, Virginia.

Discharge of Private George Cottell, Company B, 5th Massachusetts Cavalry (colored). He was born in Virginia, joined the army in the North, and was discharged in Clarksville, Texas. The 5th Massachusetts Cavalry was organized at Readville, Massachusetts, from January 9 to May 6, 1864, to serve three years. The regiment mustered out October 31, 1865. They participated in the Siege of Petersburg from June 1864 to April 1865. Five enlisted men were killed and eight wounded during this time. Cottell had his discharge folded in his wallet for many years.

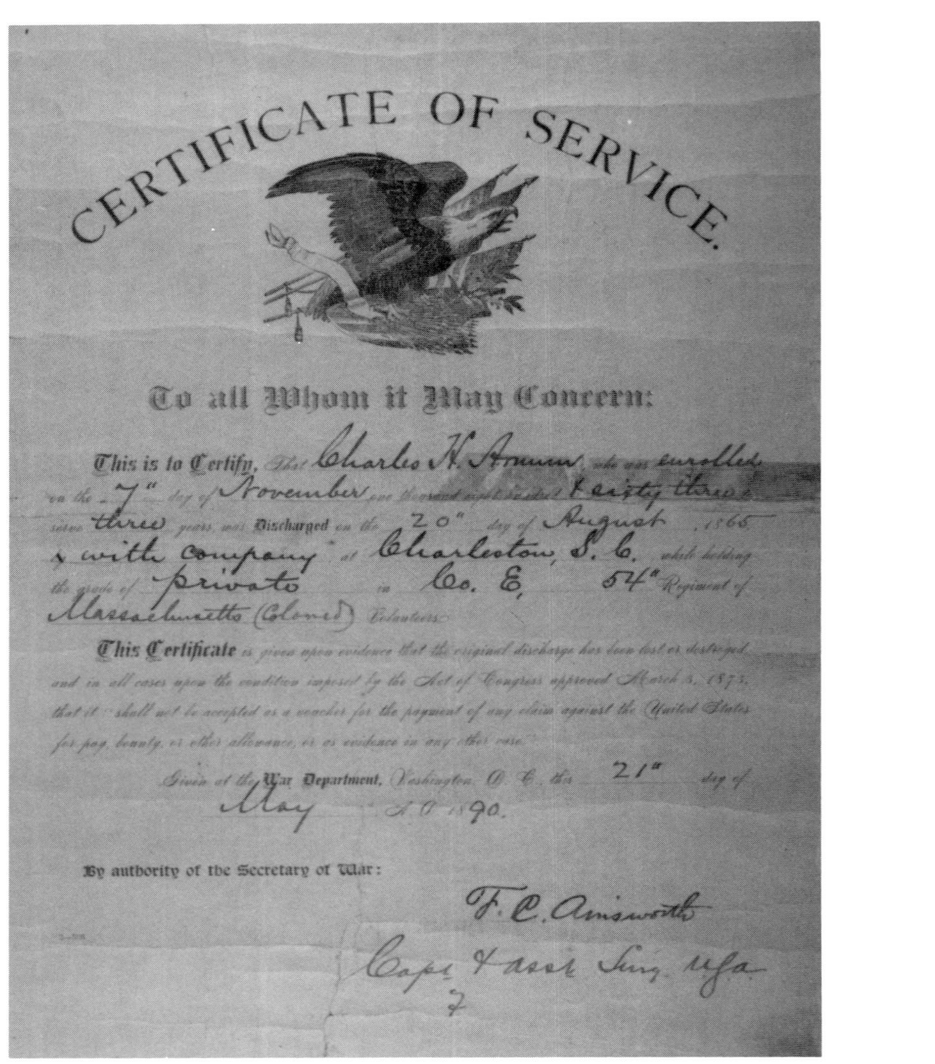

CERTIFICATE OF SERVICE.

To all Whom it May Concern:

This is to Certify, That Charles H. Arnum who was enrolled on the 7" day of November, one thousand eight hundred and sixty three to serve three years, was Discharged on the 20" day of August, 1865 with company at Charleston, S.C. while holding the grade of private in Co. E, 54" Regiment of Massachusetts (Colored) Volunteers.

This Certificate is given upon evidence that the original discharge has been lost or destroyed and in all cases upon the condition imposed by the Act of Congress approved March 3, 1873, that it shall not be accepted as a voucher for the payment of any claim against the United States for pay, bounty, or other allowance, or as evidence in any other case.

Given at the War Department, Washington, D.C. this 21" day of May A.D. 1890.

By authority of the Secretary of War:

F.C. Ainsworth
Capt & asst Surg. USA

Discharge of Private Charles H. Arussen, Company E, 54th Regiment Massachusetts (Colored) Volunteers.

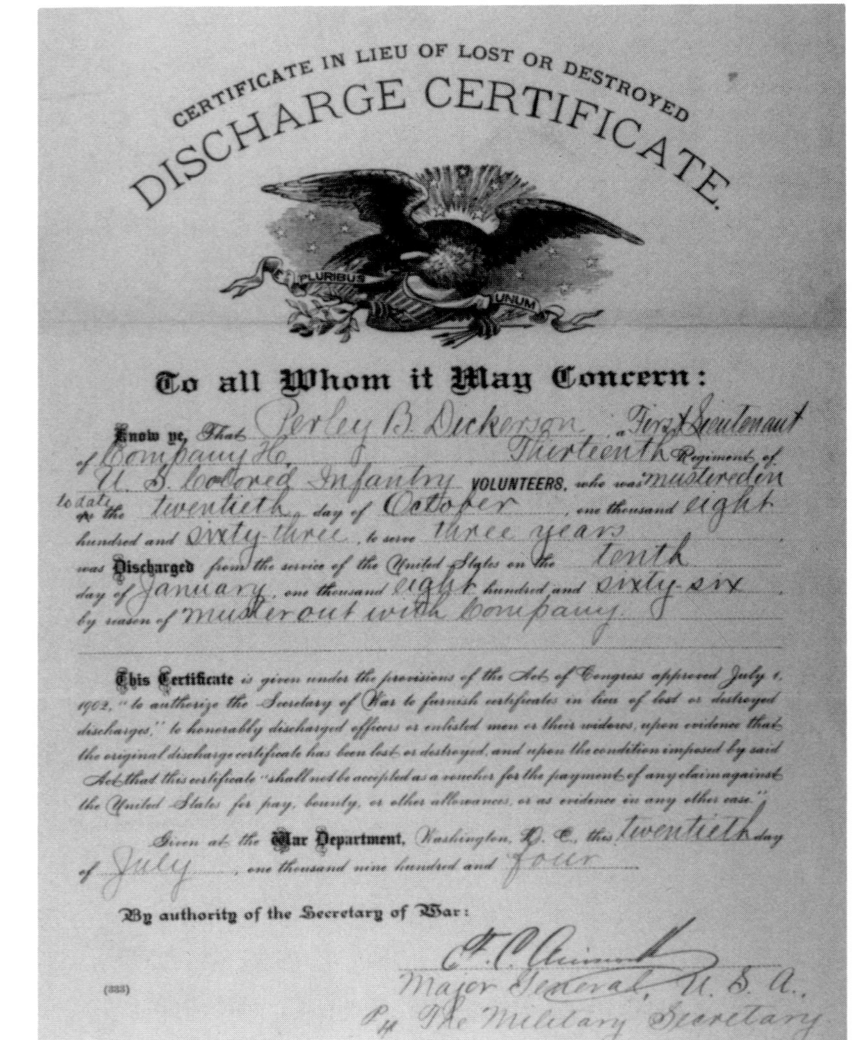

CERTIFICATE IN LIEU OF LOST OR DESTROYED
DISCHARGE CERTIFICATE.

To all Whom it May Concern:

Know ye, That Perley B. Dickerson, a First Lieutenant of Company H, Thirteenth Regiment, of U.S. Colored Infantry VOLUNTEERS, who was mustered in to date the twentieth day of October, one thousand eight hundred and sixty three, to serve three years was Discharged from the service of the United States on the tenth day of January, one thousand eight hundred and sixty six by reason of muster out with Company.

This Certificate is given under the provisions of the Act of Congress approved July 1, 1902, "to authorize the Secretary of War to furnish certificates in lieu of lost or destroyed discharges," to honorably discharged officers or enlisted men or their widows, upon evidence that the original discharge certificate has been lost or destroyed, and upon the condition imposed by said Act that this certificate "shall not be accepted as a voucher for the payment of any claim against the United States for pay, bounty, or other allowances, or as evidence in any other case."

Given at the War Department, Washington, D.C. this twentieth day of July, one thousand nine hundred and four.

By authority of the Secretary of War:

F.C. Ainsworth
Major General, U.S.A.,
The Military Secretary

(333)

Discharge of First Lieutenant Perley B. Dickerson, Company H, 13th Regiment, U.S. Colored Troops.

Discharge of Private James L. Simms, Company K, 32nd Regiment, U.S. Colored Troops. He was discharged because of physical disability. The 32nd U.S.C.T. was organized at Camp William Penn to serve three years. The regiment participated in two battles: Honey Hill and Deveux Neck, S.C. Eighteen enlisted men were killed and eighty-eight were wounded in these engagements.

Andersonville

They helped bury the dead,

The most infamous Confederate prison was Camp Sumter, commonly called "Andersonville." Also incarcerated there were about 200 black soldiers. They performed daily burial detail in the camp, picking up the dead and burying them in the cemetery.

There were 111 headstones for the colored troops who died in camp.

and they died here.

There were 776 captured colored soldiers in Confederate prison camps. They were held in Andersonville (or Camp Sumter), Salisbury, Danville, and Libby Prison. Seen here are some of the black veterans at Providence Spring, who were once prisoners of war at Andersonville, Georgia.

When It Is Over

Reminders of the greatest contribution one can give for his country. In the cemetery of many African Methodist Episcopal churchyards one can find the headstones of the Civil War veteran. Keep in mind these are in almost all cases not for the soldier who had fallen in battle but for the veteran who came home and lived out his life.

The headstone for J.W. Watts is the earlier government headstone for Civil War veterans. Private John W. Watts was drafted and mustered in Company A, 8th U.S. Colored Troops, on August 24, 1863. He was mustered out of service with his regiment on November 10, 1865.

John Edward Hopkins was mustered into service January 26, 1864, at Camp William Penn, Cheltanham Township, Pennsylvania. He was promoted to sergeant on October 29, 1864. The regiment did not engage the enemy. Hopkins was mustered out of service with his regiment December 6, 1865. This headstone is of a later period.

Rest In Peace

The three phases of the colored veteran: From the runaway slave (i.e., contraband) reaching Union lines, to his enlistment in the U.S. Colored Troops. The veteran has earned his right of citizenship. The African-American leaders felt this was most important for their people.

APPENDIX I

U.S. Colored Troops Dates of Organization and Muster-Out, States Furnishing Men, and Armament

As compiled in the *Official Army Register of the Volunteer Force of the United States Army, 1861-65,* a list of all black regiments with dates of organization and muster-out is presented below. All of these units were enlisted for a term of service of 3 years, except the 38th, 41st, 45th, 122nd, 123rd and 127th Infantry which had enlistments of 1, 2 and 3 years. A few other exceptions are noted.

The years listed under the "Armament" heading indicate the year in which a specific weapon was issued to the particular regiment. Several sources provided this information.

Unit	Date or Period of Organization	Date of Muster-Out	States Furnishing Men	Armament*
1st Cav.	Dec. 22, 1863	Feb. 4, 1866	VA	
2d Cav.	Dec. 22, 1863-Jan. 8, 1864	Feb. 12, 1866	VA	
3d Cav.	Oct. 9, 1863-Mar. 1, 1864, as 1st Miss. Cav. (A.D.)	Jan. 26, 1866	MS	
4th Cav.	Sept. 12, 1863-July 19, 1864, as 1st Cav., C. d'Afr.	Mar. 20, 1866	LA	1863: Remington .44 M1840 sabre
5th Cav.	Oct. 24-30, 1864	Mar. 16, 1866	KY	
6th Cav.	Nov. 1, 1864-June 21, 1865	Apr. 15, 1866	KY	
5th Mass. Colored Cav.	Jan. 9-May 5, 1864	Oct. 31, 1865	MA	
1st Hv. Arty.	Feb. 20-Nov. 12, 1864	Mar. 31, 1866	TN	1864: Springfield .58
3d Hv. Arty.	June 5-Dec. 22, 1863, as 1st Tenn. Hv. Arty. (A.D.)	Apr. 30, 1866	TN	1863: M1842 rifled .69 1864: Springfield .58
4th Hv. Arty.	June 16, 1863-Apr. 19, 1864, as 2d Tenn. Hv. Arty. (A.D.)	Feb. 25, 1866	MS	
5th Hv. Arty.	Aug. 7, 1863-Jan. 17, 1864, as 9th La. Volunteers (A.D.)	May 20, 1866	MS	1863: Austrian .54 1864: Springfield .58
6th Hv. Arty.	Sept. 12, 1863-Jan. 21, 1864, as 2d Miss. Hv. Arty. (A.D.)	May 13, 1866	MS	1863: Austrian .54 1864: Enfield .577 & Springfield
8th Hv. Arty.	Apr. 26-Oct. 13, 1864	Feb. 10, 1866	KY & RI	1864: Enfield .577
9th Hv. Arty.	Oct. 8-Nov. 1, 1864	Broken up May 5, 1865	TN	1864: Enfield .577
10th Hv. Arty	Nov. 29, 1862-Nov. 8, 1864, as 1st Regt., La. Hv. Arty. (A.D.)	Feb. 22, 1867	LA	1864: Enfield .577, M1863 rm
11th Hv. Arty.	Aug. 28, 1863-Jan. 25, 1864, as 14th R.I. Colored Hv. Arty.	Oct. 2, 1865	RI	Austrian .54
12th Hv. Arty.	July 15, 1864-July 15, 1865	Apr. 24, 1866	KY	1864: Enfield .577
13th Hv. Arty.	June 23, 1865	Nov. 18, 1865	KY	1864: Belgian or French rm
14th Hv. Arty.	Mar. 14, 1864-Apr. 30, 1865, as 1st N.C. Hv. Arty. (Colored)	Dec. 11, 1865	NC	1864: Enfield .577
2d Lt. Arty.				
Btry. A	April 30, 1864	Jan. 13, 1866	TN	
Btry. B	Jan. 8-Feb. 27, 1864	Mar. 17, 1866	VA	
Btry. C	Nov. 6, 1863, as 1st Btry., La. Lt. Arty. (A.D.)	Dec. 28, 1865	LA	
Btry. D	Dec. 21, 1863, as 2d Btry., La. Lt. Arty. (A.D.)	Dec. 28, 1865	LA	

Btry. E	Dec. 1, 1863, as 3d Btry., La. Lt. Arty. (A.D.)	Sept. 26, 1865	LA	
Btry. F	Nov. 23, 1863, as Memphis Lt. Btry. (A.D.)	Dec. 28, 1865	TN	
Btry. G	May 24, 1864	Aug. 12, 1865	SC	
Btry H.	June 4, 1864, as 1st Ark. Colored Btry.	Sept. 15, 1865	AR	
Btry. I	Apr. 19, 1864	Jan. 10, 1866	TN	
Independent Btry.	Dec. 23, 1864	July 22, 1865	KS	
1st Inf.	May 19-June 30, 1863	Sept. 29, 1865	DC	1863: M1842 smoothbore .69 1864: Springfield .58
2d Inf.	June 23-Nov. 11, 1863	Jan. 5, 1866	VA	1863: M1842 smoothbore .69 1864: Springfield & Enfield
3d Inf.	Aug. 3-10, 1863	Oct. 31, 1865	PA	1863: Springfield .58
4th Inf.	July 15-Sept. 1, 1863	May 4, 1866	MD	1863: Enfield & Springfield
5th Inf.	Aug. 6, 1863-Jan. 15, 1864, as 127th Ohio Inf.	Sept. 20, 1865	OH	1863: Springfield .58
6th Inf.	July 28-Sept. 12, 1863	Sept. 20, 1865	PA	1863: Springfield .58
7th Inf.	Sept. 26-Nov. 12, 1863	Oct. 13, 1866	MD	1863: Springfield & Enfield
8th Inf.	Sept. 22-Dec. 4, 1863	Nov. 10, 1865	PA	1863: Springfield .58
9th Inf.	Nov. 11-30, 1863	Nov. 26, 1866	MD	1863: Enfield & Springfield
10th Inf.	Nov. 18, 1863-Sept. 23, 1864	May 17, 1866	VA	1863: Enfield .577
11th Inf. (old)	Dec. 19, 1863-Sept. 23, 1864	Consolidated with 113th Regt., Apr. 22, 1865	AR	1864: Springfield & Enfield
11th Inf. (new)	June 20, 1863-Apr. 2, 1864, as 1st Ala. Siege Arty. (A.D.)	Jan. 12, 1866	AL	1864: Springfield .58
12th Inf.	July 24-Aug. 14, 1863	Jan. 16, 1866	TN	1863: M1842 rifled .69 1864: Enfield .577
13th Inf.	Nov. 19, 1863	Jan. 10, 1866	TN	1863: altered muskets 1864: Enfield .577
14th Inf.	Nov. 16, 1863-Jan. 8, 1864	Mar. 26, 1866	TN	1863: altered muskets 1864: Enfield .577
15th Inf.	Dec. 2, 1863-Mar. 11, 1864	Apr. 7, 1866	TN	1863: altered muskets
16th Inf.	Dec. 4, 1863-Feb. 13, 1864	Apr. 30, 1866	TN	1863: M1842 rifled .69
17th Inf.	Dec. 12-21, 1863	Apr. 25, 1866	TN	1863: M1842 rifled .69
18th Inf.	Feb. 1-Sept. 28, 1864	Feb. 21, 1866	MO	1864: Enfield .577
19th Inf.	Dec. 25, 1863-Jan. 16, 1864	Jan. 15, 1867	MD	1864: Enfield & Springfield
20th Inf.	Feb. 9, 1864	Oct. 7, 1865	NY	1864: Enfield .577
21st Inf.	June 19, 1863-Oct. 1, 1864, as 3d & 4th S.C.	Apr. 25, 1866	SC	1864: Springfield .58
22d Inf.	Jan. 10-29, 1864	Oct. 16, 1865	PA	1863: Springfield .58
23d Inf.	Nov. 23, 1863-June 30, 1864	Nov. 30, 1865	VA	1863: Enfield .577 1864: Springfield .58
24th Inf.	Jan. 30-Mar. 30, 1865	Oct. 1, 1865	PA	
25th Inf.	Jan. 13-Feb. 12, 1864	Dec. 6, 1865	PA	1864: Enfield .577
26th Inf.	Feb. 27, 1864	Aug. 28, 1865	NY	1864: Enfield .577
27th Inf.	Jan. 16-Aug. 6, 1864	Sept. 21, 1865	OH	1864: Springfield & Enfield
28th Inf.	Dec. 24, 1863-Mar. 31, 1864	Nov. 8, 1865	IN	1864: Springfield .58

29th Inf.	6 companies organized Apr. 24, 1864; 4 companies organized Oct. 23, 1864-Jan. 1, 1865	Nov. 6, 1865	IL	1864: Springfield .58
30th Inf.	Feb. 12-Mar. 18, 1864	Dec. 10, 1865	MD	1864: Enfield & Springfield
31st Inf.	Apr. 29-Nov. 14, 1864, as 30th Conn. Colored Volunteers	Nov. 7, 1865	NY	1864: Springfield .58
32d Inf.	Feb. 17-Mar. 7, 1864	Aug. 22, 1865	PA	1864: Enfield & Springfield
33d Inf.	Jan. 31, 1863, as 1st S.C. Volunteers (A.D.)	Jan. 31, 1866	SC	1863: Austrian & Prussian rm 1864: Belgian & French rm
34th Inf.	May 22, 1863-Dec. 31, 1864, as 2d S.C. Colored Volunteers	Feb. 28, 1866	SC	1863: foreign smoothbores 1864: Enfield .577
35th Inf.	June 30, 1863, as 1st N.C. Volunteers	June 1, 1866	NC	1863: Enfield .577 1864: M1863 rifled musket .58
36th Inf.	Oct. 28, 1863, as 2d N.C. Colored Volunteers	Oct. 28, 1866	NC	1864: Enfield .577
37th Inf.	Jan. 30-Sept. 19, 1864, as 3d N.C. Volunteers	Feb. 11, 1867	NC	1863: Enfield .577 1864: M1863 rifled musket .58
38th Inf.	Jan. 23, 1864-Mar. 30, 1865	Jan. 25, 1867	VA	
39th Inf.	Mar. 22-31, 1864	Dec. 4, 1865	MD	1864: Springfield .58
40th Inf.	Feb. 29, 1864-May 6, 1865	Apr. 25, 1866	TN	1864: Enfield .577, M1842 rifled and smoothbore .69
41st Inf. (Bn. of)	Sept. 30-Dec. 7, 1864	Dec. 10, 1865	PA	1864: Springfield .58
42d Inf.	April 20, 1864-July 6, 1865	Jan. 31, 1866	TN	1864: Enfield .577
43d Inf.	Mar. 12-June 3, 1864	Oct. 20, 1865	PA	1864: Springfield .58
44th Inf.	Apr. 7-Sept. 16, 1864	Apr. 30, 1866	GA	1864: Springfield .58
45th Inf.	June 13-Aug. 19, 1864	Nov. 4, 1865	PA	1864: Springfield .58
46th Inf.	May 1, 1863, as 1st Ark. Volunteers (A.D.)	Jan. 30, 1866	AR	1863: Austrian .54
47th Inf.	May 5, 1863, as 8th La. Volunteers (A.D.)	Jan. 5, 1866	LA	1863: Austrian .58 1864: M1863 rifled musket .58
48th Inf.	May 6-Aug. 8, 1863, as 10th La. Volunteers (A.D.)	Jan. 4, 1866	LA	1863: Austrian .54 1864: M1863 rifled musket .58
49th Inf.	May 23-Aug. 22, 1863, as 11th La. Volunteers (A.D.)	Mar. 22, 1866	LA	1863: Austrian .54 1864: M1863 rifled musket .58
50th Inf.	July 11-27, 1863, as 12th La. Volunteers (A.D.)	Mar. 20, 1866	LA	1863: Enfield .577 1864: M1863 rifled musket .58
51st Inf.	May 16, 1863-Mar. 7, 1864, as 1st Miss. Volunteers (A.D.)	June 16, 1866	MS	1863: Austrian .54 1864: Springfield .58
52d Inf.	July 27-Dec. 22, 1863, as 2d Miss. Volunteers (A.D.)	May 5, 1866	MS	1863: Enfield .577 1864: Springfield .58
53d Inf.	May 19, 1863, as 3d Miss. Volunteers (A.D.)	Mar. 8, 1866	MS	
54th Inf.	Sept. 4-Dec. 25, 1863, as 2d Ark. Volunteers (A.D.)	Dec. 31, 1866	AR	1863: M1840 rifle & .69 smooth 1864: Springfield, Enfield & foriegn rifled muskets
55th Inf.	May 21, 1863, as 1st Ala. Volunteers (A.D.)	Dec. 31, 1866	AL	1863: Enfield .577 1864: Springfield .58
56th Inf.	Aug. 12-Sept. 29, 1863, as 3d Ark. Volunteers (A.D.)	Sept. 15, 1866	AR	1864: Enfield .577
57th Inf.	Dec. 2, 1863-Mar. 1, 1864, as 4th Ark. Volunteers (A.D.)	Dec. 13, 1866	AR	1864: Enfield .577

58th Inf.	Aug. 27, 1863, as 6th Miss. Volunteers (A.D.)	Apr. 30, 1866	MS	1863: Enfield .577 1864: Springfield .58
59th Inf.	June 6-27, 1863, as 1st Tenn. Volunteers (A.D.)	Jan. 31, 1866	TN	1863: Enfield & Springfield
60th Inf.	Oct. 15-Dec. 4, 1863, as 1st Iowa Volunteers (A.D.)	Oct. 15, 1865	IA	1863: Enfield .577
61st Inf.	June 30-Aug. 8, 1863, as 2d Tenn. Volunteers (A.D.)	Dec. 30, 1865	TN	1863: Enfield .577
62d Inf.	Dec. 7-14, 1863, as 1st Mo. Volunteers (A.D.)	Mar. 31, 1866	MO	1864: Enfield .577
63d Inf.	Nov. 19-Dec. 14, 1863, as 9th La. Volunteers (A.D.)	Jan. 9, 1866	LA	1863: Enfield .577 & Austrian .54 1864: M1863 rifled musket
64th Inf.	Dec. 1, 1863-Feb. 1, 1864 as 7th La. Volunteers (A.D.)	Mar. 13, 1866	LA	1864: Enfield .577
65th Inf.	Dec. 18, 1863-Jan. 16, 1864, as 2d Mo. Volunteers (A.D.)	Jan. 8, 1867	MO	1864: Enfield .577
66th Inf.	Dec. 11, 1863-Jan. 11, 1864, as 4th Miss. Volunteers (A.D.)	Mar. 20, 1866	MS	1863: Springfield & Enfield
67th Inf.	Jan. 19-Feb. 13, 1864, 3d Mo. Volunteers (A.D.)	July 12, 1865	MO	1864: Enfield .577
68th Inf.	Mar. 8-Apr. 23, 1864, as 4th Mo. Volunteers (A.D.)	Feb. 5, 1866	MO	1864: Enfield .577
69th Inf.	Dec. 14, 1864-Mar. 17, 1865	Discontinued September 20, 1865	AR	1864: Enfield .577
70th Inf.	Apr. 23-Oct. 1, 1864	Mar. 7, 1866	MS	1864: Enfield .577
71st Inf.	Mar. 3-Aug. 13, 1864	Nov. 8, 1864	MS	
72d Inf.	Apr. 18-22, 1865	Discontinued May 3, 1865	KY	
73d Inf.	Sept. 27, 1862, as 1st La. Native Guards (A.D.)	Mustered-out when terms of service expired	LA	1862: Enfield .577 1864: M1863 rifled musket
74th Inf.	Oct. 12, 1862, as 2d La. Native Guards (A.D.)	Oct. 11, 1865	LA	1862: Enfield .577 & M1842 smoothbore .69
75th Inf.	Nov. 24,1862, as 3d La. Native Guards (A.D.)	Nov. 25, 1865	LA	1862: Austrian .54 1864: M1863 rifled musket
76th Inf.	Feb. 10-Mar. 6, 1863, as 4th La. Native Guards (A.D.)	Dec. 31, 1865	LA	
77th Inf.	Dec. 8, 1863, as 5th Inf., C. d'Afr.	Consolidated with 10th U.S. Colored Hv.Arty., Oct. 1, 1865	LA	1863: Austrian .54
78th Inf.	Sept. 4, 1863, as 6th Inf., C. d'Afr.	Jan. 6, 1866	LA	1863: M1842 smoothbore .69
79th Inf. (old)	Aug. 31, 1863, as 7th Inf. C. d'Afr.	Broken up July 28, 1864	LA	
79th Inf. (new)	Jan. 13-May 2, 1863, as 1st Kans. Colored Volunteers	Oct. 1, 1865	KS	1863: converted muskets
80th Inf.	Sept. 1, 1863, 8th Inf. C. d'Afr.	Mar. 1, 1867	LA	1863: M1842 smoothbore .69 1864: Enfield .577
81st Inf.	Sept. 2, 1863, as 9th Inf. C. d'Afr.	Nov. 30, 1866	LA	1863: M1842 smoothbore .69 1864: Enfield .577
82d Inf.	Sept. 1, 1863, as 10th Inf. C. d'Afr.	Sept. 10, 1866	LA	1863: M1842 smoothbore .69

83d Inf. (old)	Aug. 17, 1863, as 11th Inf. C. d'Afr.	Broken up July 28, 1864	LA	1863: M1842 smooth & Springfield .58 1864: Enfield .577
83d Inf. (new)	Aug. 11-Oct. 17, 1863, as 2d Kans. Colored Volunteers	Oct. 9, 1865	KS	1863: Enfield .577
84th Inf.	Sept. 24-Oct. 16, 1863, as 12th Inf., C. d'Afr.	Mar. 14, 1866	LA	1863: Austrian .54
85th Inf.	Mar. 11, 1864, as 13th Inf. C. d'Afr.	Consolidated with 77th U.S. Colored Inf., May 24, 1864	LA	
86th Inf.	Aug. 12-Sept. 3, 1863, as 14th Inf., C. d'Afr.	Apr. 10, 1866	LA	1863: converted muskets 1864: M1863 rifled musket & Enfield .577
87th Inf. (old)	Oct. 8-16, 1863, as 16th Inf., C. d'Afr.	Subsequently changed to 87th U.S. Colored Inf. (new), Dec. 19, 1864	LA	1863: converted muskets 1864: Enfield .577
87th Inf. (new)	Nov. 26, 1864, as 81st U.S. Colored Inf. (new)' designated 87th U.S. Colored Inf. (new) on Dec. 19, 1864	Consolidated with 84th U.S. Colored Inf., Aug. 14, 1865	LA	1863: converted muskets 1864: Enfield .577
88th Inf. (old)	Sept. 24, 1863, as 17th Inf., C. d'Afr.	Broken up July 28, 1864	LA	1863: M1842 smoothbore .69
88th Inf. (new)	Feb. 20-Aug. 10, 1865	Consolidated with 3d U.S. Colored Hv. Arty., Dec. 16, 1865	TN	
89th Inf	Oct. 9-Nov. 8, 1863, as 18th Inf., C. d'Afr.	Broken up July 28, 1864	LA	1863: M1842 smoothbore .69 & Enfield .577
90th Inf.	Feb. 11, 1864, as 19th Inf., C. d'Afr.	Broken up July 28, 1864	LA	1863: Enfield .577
91st Inf.	Sept. 1, 1863, as 20th Inf., C. d'Afr.	Consolidated with 74th U.S. Colored Inf., July 7, 1864	LA	1863: Enfield .577
92d Inf.	Sept. 30-Oct. 24, 1863, as 22d Inf., C. d'Afr.	Dec. 31, 1865	LA	1863: converted muskets 1864: M1863 rifled musket
93d Inf.	Nov. 21, 1863, as 25th Inf., C. d'Afr.	Broken up June 23, 1865	LA	1863: converted muskets 1864: M1863 rifled musket
95th Inf.	Apr. 28, 1863, as 1st Engineers, C. d'Afr.	Consolidated with 87th U.S. Colored Inf. to form 81st U.S. Colored Inf., Nov. 26, 1864	LA	1863: Belgian & French rifled musket
96th Inf.	Aug. 15, 1863, as 2d Engineers, C. d'Afr.	Jan. 29, 1866	LA	1863: converted muskets
97th Inf.	Aug. 26, 1863, as 3d Engineers, C.d'Afr.	Apr. 6, 1866	LA	1863: Belgian & French rm 1864: M1863 rifled musket
98th Inf.	Sept. 3, 1863-Mar. 3, 1864, as 4th Engineers, C. d'Afr.	Consolidated with 78th Regt., Aug. 26, 1865	LA	1863: converted muskets 1864: M1863 rifled musket
99th Inf. (Bn. of)	Aug. 27, 1863, as 15th Inf., C. d'Afr.	Apr. 23, 1866	LA	1863: converted muskets 1864: M1863 rifled musket
100th Inf.	May 3-June 1, 1864	Dec. 26, 1865	KY	1864: Enfield .577
101st Inf.	Sept. 16, 1864-Aug. 5, 1865	Jan. 21, 1866	TN	1864: altered muskets

102d Inf.	Feb. 17, 1864, as 1st Mich. Colored Volunteers	Sept. 30, 1865	MI	Austrian .58, later M1863 rifled musket
103d Inf.	Mar. 10, 1865	Apr. 15-20, 1866	SC	
104th Inf.	Apr. 28-June 25, 1865	Feb. 5, 1866	SC	
106th Inf.	Mar. 31-Aug. 10, 1864, as 4th Ala. Inf. (A.D.)	Condolidated with 40th U.S.Colored Inf., Nov. 7, 1865	AL	1864: Springfield .58
107th Inf.	May 3-Sept. 15, 1864	Nov. 22, 1866	KY	1864: Springfield .58
108th Inf.	June 20-Aug. 22, 1864	Mar. 21, 1866	KY	1864: Enfield .577
109th Inf.	July 5, 1864	Feb. 6, 1866	KY	1864: Enfield .577
110th Inf.	Nov. 20, 1863-Jan. 14, 1864, as 2d Ala. Volunteers (A.D.)	Feb. 6, 1866	AL	1864: Enfield .577
111th Inf.	Jan. 13-Apr. 5, 1864, as 3d Regt., Ala. Volunteers (A.D.)	Apr. 30, 1866	AL	1864: M1842 rifled .69
112th Inf.	Apr. 23-Nov. 8, 1864	Consolidated with 11th U.S. Colored Inf. (old) to form 113th U.S. Colored Inf. (new), Apr. 1, 1865	AR	1864: Enfield .577
113th Inf. (old)	Mar. 1-June 20, 1864, as 6th Ark. Volunteers (A.D.)	Consolidated with 11th U.S. Colored Inf. and 112th U.S. Colored Inf. to form 113th U.S. Colored Inf. (new) on April 1, 1865	AR	
113th Inf. (new)	Apr. 1, 1865, by consolidation of the 11th (old), 112th, and 113th (old) U.S. Colored Infantries	Apr. 9, 1866	AR	1864: Enfield .577
114th Inf.	July 4, 1864	Apr. 2, 1867	KY	1864: Enfield .577
115th Inf.	July 15-Oct. 21, 1864	Feb. 10, 1866	KY	1864: Enfield .577
116th Inf.	June 6-July 12, 1864	Jan. 17, 1867	KY	1864: Enfield .577
117th Inf.	July 18-Sept. 27, 1864	Aug. 10, 1867	KY	1864: Enfield .577
118th Inf.	Oct. 19, 1864	Feb. 6, 1866	KY	1864: Enfield .577
119th Inf.	Jan. 18-May 16, 1865	Apr. 27, 1866	KY	1864: Enfield .577
120th Inf.	Nov. 1864-June 1865	Discontinued June 21, 1865	KY	1864: Enfield .577
121st Inf.	Oct. 8, 1864-May 31, 1865	Discontinued June 30, 1865	KY	1864: Enfield .577
122d Inf. (Bn. of)	Dec. 31, 1864	Feb. 8, 1866	KY	1864: Enfield .577
123d Inf.	Dec. 2, 1864	Oct. 16, 1865	KY	1864: Enfield .577
124th Inf.	Jan. 1-Apr. 27, 1865	Oct. 24, 1865	KY	
125th Inf.	Feb. 13-June 2, 1865	Oct. 31, 1867-Dec. 20, 1867	KY	
127th Inf. (Bn.)	Aug. 23-Sept. 10, 1864	Oct. 20, 1865	PA	1864: Springfield .58
128th Inf.	Apr. 23-29, 1865	Oct. 10, 1866	SC	
135th Inf.	Mar. 28, 1865	Oct. 23, 1865	NC	
136th Inf.	July 15, 1865	Jan. 4, 1866	GA	

137th Inf.	Enrolled Apr. 8, 1865; mustered into U.S. service June 1, 1865	Jan. 15, 1866	GA	
138th Inf.	July 15, 1865	Jan. 6, 1866	GA	
54th Mass. Colored Inf.	Mar. 30-May 13, 1863	Aug. 20, 1865	MA	1863: Enfield .577
55th Mass. Colored Inf.	May 31-June 22, 1863	Aug. 29, 1865	MA	1863: Enfield .577
29th Conn. Colored Inf.	Mar. 8, 1864	Oct. 24, 1865	CT	1864: Enfield .577
6th La. Colored Inf. (60 days)	July 4, 1863	Aug. 13, 1863	LA	
7th La. Colored Inf.	July 10, 1863	Aug. 6, 1863	LA	
Company A, unassigned (1 year)	Sept. 28, 1864	July 29, 1865	VA	
Independent Company A (100 days)	July 20, 1864	Nov. 14, 1864	PA	

*To conserve space, certain abbreviations have been used:

Enfield or Enfield .577 = Enfield rifles or rifled muskets .577 cal., P1853

Springfield or Springfield .58 = M1855 or M1861 Harpers Ferry or Springfield rifled muskets or other regulation US rifled muskets .58 cal.

M1863 rm or M1863 rifled musket = M1863 Springfield rifled muskets .58 cal.

Austrian .54 = Austrian rifled muskets .54 or .55 cal.

M1842 rifled .69 = M1842 Springfield or other regulation US rifled muskets .69 cal.

M1842 smoothbore .69 = M1842 Springfield smoothbore muskets .69 cal.

altered or converted muskets = generally, .69 cal. smoothbore muskets that may have been originally flintlock weapons.

Remington .44 = M1861 Remington Army revolver .44 cal.

rm = rifled musket

APPENDIX II

The United States Colored Troops were assigned to the following Army Corps.

Army Corps	Insignia	Brigade	Division
7th		2nd 1st 2nd	1st 2nd Frontier
9th		1st 2nd	4th 4th
10th		1st 2nd 3rd	3rd 3rd 3rd
13th	no badge adopted	Engineer	
16th		1st 2nd	4th 4th
18th		1st 2nd 3rd	3rd 3rd 3rd
22nd		Martingdale's Provisional	
23rd			5th
25th		2nd 3rd 1st 2nd 3rd 2nd 3rd	1st 1st 2nd 2nd 2nd 3rd 3rd

APPENDIX III

U.S.C.T. Draft Rendezvous Encampments

Camp Casey, Virginia
Infantry: 23rd

Camp Hamilton, Virginia
Cavalry: 1st

Hart's Island, New York City
Infantry: 31st

Camp Holly Springs, Louisiana
Infantry: 64th

Camp Jim Lane, near Wyandot, Missouri
Infantry: 1st Kansas Colored

Camp Parapet, Louisiana
Infantry: 95th

Camp Saxton, South Carolina
Infantry: 1st South Carolina

Camp Strong Station, New Orleans, Louisiana
Infantry: 1st, 2nd and 3rd Louisiana Native Guards

Fort Monroe, Virginia
Cavalry: 2nd

Fort Smith, Arkansas
Infantry: 11th (old)

Camp William Penn, Cheltanham Township, Pennsylvania
Infantry: 3rd, 6th, 8th, 22nd, 24th, 25th, 32nd, 41st, 43rd, 45th, and 127th

Independent Company (100 days)

Camp Nelson, Kentucky
Cavalry: 5th and 6th

Heavy Artillery: 12th and 13th

Infantry: 114th, 116th, 119th and 124th

Camp Stanton, Bryanton, Maryland
Infantry: 9th, 19th and 30th

Benton Barracks, Missouri
Infantry: 60th, 62nd, 65th and 68th

Fort Scott, Arkansas
Infantry: 79th (new) and 83rd (new)

Camp Delaware, Ohio
Infantry: 5th and 27th

Rikers Island, New York City
Infantry: 20th and 26th

Camp Birney, Baltimore, Maryland
Infantry: 4th, 7th and 39th

APPENDIX IV

Black Officers in the Civil War

As nearly as can be determined from military service records, the following list includes all the black commissioned officers who served in black regiments during the Civil War.*

1st Louisiana Native Guards (subsequently designated 73rd USCI).

Captains: Alfred Bourgeau, Andrew Calloux, Edward Carter, John DePass, Joseph Follin, James H. Ingraham, Alcide Lewis, Jame Lewis, Henry L. Rey.

Lieutenants: Emile Detiege, William Harding, Louis D. Larrien, Victor Lavigne, Jules Mallet, Morris W. Morris, Ehurd Moss, Oscar Orillion, Paul Poree, Eugene Rapp, Henry Louis Rey, Charles Sentmanat, Hyppolite St. Louis, Louis A. Thibant, Charles Warfield.

2nd Louisiana Native Guards (subsequently designated 74th USCI)
Major: Francis E. Dumas.

Captains: William B. Barrett, William Belley, Arnold Bertonneau, Hannibal Carter, Edward P. Chase, Robert H. Isabelle, P.B.S. Pinchback, Samuel W. Ringgold, Joseph Villeverde, Samuel J. Wilkinson.

Lieutenants: Alfred Annis, Jr., Louis De Gray, Peter O. Depremond, Alphonso Fleury, Jr., Calvin B. Glover, Solomon Hayes, Ernest Hubeau, Joseph Jones, Rufus Kinsley, John W. Latting, Jules P. Lewis, Theodore A. Martin, Ernest Murphy, Octave Rey, Jasper Thompson, Frank L. Trask, George R. Watson, Joseph Wellington.

3rd Louisiana Native Guards (subsequently designated 75th USCI)

Captains: Leon G. Forstall, Peter A. Gardener, Charles W. Gibbons, Jacques A. Gla, John C. Holland, Samuel Laurence, Joseph B. Oliver.

Lieutenants: Alfred Bourgeau, Charles Butler, Chester W. Converse, Octave Foy, William Hardin, Valdes Lessassier, Ernest Longpre, Jr., G.B. Miller, James E. Moore, E.T. Nash, Joseph G. Parker, Louis Petit, Hypolite Ray, Charles Schermerhorn, G.W. Talmon, A.F. Tervalon.

54th Massachusetts Volunteer Infantry

Lieutenants: Stephen A. Swails, Peter Vogelsang, Frank M. Welch.

55th Massachusetts Volunteer Infantry

Lieutenants: John F. Shorter, James M. Trotter, William H. Dupree.

104th U.S. Colored Infantry

Major: Martin R. Delany

Captain: O.S.B. Wall

Independent Battery, U.S. Colored Light Artillery

Captain: H. Ford Douglas

Lieutenants: William D. Mathews, Patrick H. Minor

Surgeons: Anderson R. Abbott, Alexander T. Augusta, John V. De Grasse, William B. Ellis, William Powell, Charles B. Purvis, John Rapier, Alpheus Tucker.

Chaplains: Jeremiah Asher, John R. Bowles, Francis A. Boyd, Samuel Harrison, William H. Hunter, William Jackson, Chauncey B. Leonard, George W. Levere, Benjamin F. Randolph, David Stevens, Henry M. Turner, James Underdue, William Waring, Garland H. White.

*Berlin, Ira. *Freedom, Vol. II, The Black Military Experience.*

APPENDIX V

White Officers who received the Medal of Honor leading Colored Troops*

1. Appelton, William	1st Lieutenant	4th
2. Barrell, Charles	1st Lieutenant	102nd
3. Bates, Delevan	Colonel	30th
4. Bennett, Orson	1st Lieutenant	102nd
5. Brush, George	1st Lieutenant	34th
6. Davidson, Andrew	1st Lieutenant	30th
7. Edgerton, Nathan	1st Lieutenant	6th
8. Ellsworth, Thomas	Captain	55th Mass. Vol.
9. Evans, Ira H.	Captain	116th
10. Merriam, Henry C.	Lieutenant Colonel	73rd
11. Nichols, Henry	2nd Lieutenant	73rd
12. Thorn, Walter	2nd Lieutenant	116th
13. Wright, Albert	Captain	43rd

*Committee on Veterans' Affairs, United States Senate.
Medal of Honor Recipients, 1863-1978. U.S. Govt. Printing Office, 1979.

APPENDIX VI

Sutlers with the United States Colored Troops*

CAVALRY

1 Regt.	J.W. Chronister
	John Paul Jones
2 Regt.	W. Stewart

INFANTRY

1 Regt.	George Seaton
2 Regt.	Stewart Wellington
4 Regt.	R.J. Bowdin
	W.C. Cooper
	G.W. Skiff
5 Regt.	Henry P. Elias
	R.D. Kuhn
6 Regt.	William B. Brisben
7 Regt.	John H. Butler
8 Regt.	E.A. Rogers
9 Regt.	A.C. James
14 Regt.	Ellis J. Peer
19 Regt.	J.B. Putnam
22 Regt.	L.O. Cameron
23 Regt.	O.A. Morse
27 Regt.	____________
29 Regt.	C.S. Hawley
31 Regt.	George H. Josselyn
36 Regt.	Henry B. Walker
	Charles Wilbur
38 Regt.	Richard North
	Frank Stenens
41 Regt.	L.C. Gordon
48 Regt.	____________
107 Regt.	Temple Reamer
109 Regt.	Marion L. Bouser
116 Regt.	E.R. Felton
117 Regt.	C.H. Smith
118 Regt.	S.S. Linton
119 Regt.	J.M. Longwell
127 Regt.	S.S. Mann

*Lord, Francis A. *Civil War Sutlers and Their Wares.*

APPENDIX VII

Index of Battles

As compiled in the *Official Army Register of the Volunteer Force of the United States Army, 1861-65,* Part VIII, United States Colored Troops and other black units took part in the following battles and skirmishes during the Civil War.

"ALLIANCE," STEAMER, FLA.
(March 8, 1865)
U.S.C.T.— 99th inf.

AMITE RIVER, LA.
(March 18, 1865)
U.S.C.T.— 77th inf.

APPOMATTOX COURT HOUSE, VA.
(April 9, 1865)
U.S.C.T.— 41st inf.

ARKANSAS RIVER, ARK.
(Dec. 18, 1864)
U.S.C.T.— 54th inf.

ASH BAYOU, LA.
(Nov. 19, 1864)
U.S.C.T.— 93rd inf.

ASHEPOO RIVER, S.C.
(May 16, 1864)
U.S.C.T.— 34th inf.

ASHWOOD, MISS.
(June 25, 1864)
U.S.C.T.— 63rd inf.

ASHWOOD LANDING, LA.
(May 1 and 4, 1864)
U.S.C.T.— 64th inf.

ATHENS, ALA.
(Sept. 24, 1864)
U.S.C.T.— 106th, 110th and 111th inf.

BARRANCAS, FLA.
(July 22, 1864)
U.S.C.T.— 82d inf.

BAXTER'S SPRINGS, KAN.
(Oct. 6, 1863)
U.S.C.T.— 83d (new) inf.

BAYOU BIDELL, LA.
(Oct. 15, 1864)
U.S.C.T.— 52d inf.

BAYOU BOEUF, ARK.
(Dec. 13, 1863)
U.S.C.T.— 3d cav.

BAYOU MASON, MISS.
(July--, 1864)
U.S.C.T.— 66th inf.

BAYOU ST. LOUIS, MISS.
(Nov. 17, 1863)
U.S.C.T.— 91st inf.

BAYOU TENSAS, LA.
(Aug. 10, 1863)
U.S.C.T.— 48th inf.

BAYOU TENSAS, LA.
(July 30 and Aug. 26, 1864)
U.S.C.T.— 66th inf.

BAYOU TUNICA, LA.
(Nov. 9, 1863)
U.S.C.T.— 73d inf.

BERMUDA HUNDRED, VA.
(May 4, 1864)
U.S.C.T.— 4th inf.

BERMUDA HUNDRED, VA.
(May 20, 1864)
U.S.C.T.— 1st cav.

BERMUDA HUNDRED, VA.
(Aug. 24 and 25, 1864)
U.S.C.T.— 7th inf.

BERMUDA HUNDRED, VA.
(Nov. 30 and Dec. 4, 1864)
U.S.C.T.— 19th inf.

BERMUDA HUNDRED, VA.
(Dec. 1, 1864)
U.S.C.T.— 39th inf.

BERMUDA HUNDRED, VA.
(Dec. 13, 1864)
U.S.C.T.— 23d inf.

BERWICK, LA.
(April 26, 1864)
U.S.C.T.— 98th inf.

BIG CREEK, ARK.
(July 26, 1864)
U.S.C.T.— Batt'y E, 2d lt. art., 60th inf.

BIG SPRINGS, KY.
(Jan.--, 1865)
U.S.C.T.— 12th hy. art.

BLACK CREEK, FLA.
(July 27, 1864)
U.S.C.T.— 35th inf.

BLACK RIVER, LA.
(Nov. 1, 1864)
U.S.C.T.— 6th hy. art.

BOGGS' MILLS, ARK.
(Jan. 24, 1865)
U.S.C.T.— 11th (old) inf.

BOYD'S STATION, ALA.
(March 18, 1865)
U.S.C.T.— 101st inf.

BOYKIN'S MILL, S.C.
(April 18, 1865)
U.S.C.T.— 54th (Mass.) inf.

BRADFORD'S SPRINGS, S.C.
(April 18, 1865)
U.S.C.T.— 102d inf.

BRAWLEY FORK, TENN.
(March 25, 1865)
U.S.C.T.— 17th inf.

BRICE'S CROSS ROADS, MISS.
(June 10, 1864)
U.S.C.T.— Batt'y F, 2d lt. art.; 55th & 59th inf.

BRIGGEN CREEK, S.C.
(Feb. 25, 1865)
U.S.C.T.— 55th (Mass.) inf.

BRYANT'S PLANTATION, FLA.
(Oct. 21, 1864)
U.S.C.T.— 3d inf.

CABIN CREEK, C.N.
(July 1 and 2, 1863)
U.S.C.T.— 79th (new) inf.

CABIN CREEK, C.N.
(Nov. 4, 1865)
U.S.C.T.— 54th inf.

CABIN POINT, VA.
(Aug. 5, 1864)
U.S.C.T.— 1st cav.

CAMDEN, ARK.
(April 24, 1864)
U.S.C.T.— 57th inf.

CAMP MARENGO, LA.
(Sept. 14, 1864)
U.S.C.T.— 63d inf.

CEDAR KEYS, FLA.
(Feb. 16, 1865)
U.S.C.T.— 2d inf.

CHAPIN'S FARM, VA.
(Sept. 29 and 30, 1864)
U.S.C.T.— 2d cav.; 1st, 4th, 5th, 6th, 7th, 8th, 9th, 22d, 29th, (Conn.,) 36th, 37th, and 38th inf.

CHAPIN'S FARM, VA.
(Nov. 4, 1864)
U.S.C.T.— 22d inf.

CHATTANOOGA, TENN.
(Feb.--, 1865)
U.S.C.T.— 16th inf.

"CHIPPEWIA," STEAMER, ARK.
(Feb. 17, 1865)
U.S.C.T.— 83d (new) inf.

"CITY BELLE," STEAMER, LA.
(May 3, 1864)
U.S.C.T.— 73d inf.

CITY POINT, VA.
(May 6, 1864)
U.S.C.T.— 5th inf.

CITY POINT, VA.
(June--, 1864)
U.S.C.T.— Batt'y B, 2d lt. art.

CLARKSVILLE, ARK.
(Jan. 18, 1865)
U.S.C.T.— 79th (new) inf.

CLINTON, LA.
(Aug. 25, 1864)
U.S.C.T.— 4th cav.

COLEMAN'S PLANTATION, MISS.
(July 4, 1864)
U.S.C.T.— 52d inf.

COLUMBIA, LA.
(Feb. 4, 1864)
U.S.C.T.— 66th inf.

CONCORDIA BAYOU, LA.
(Aug. 5, 1864)
U.S.C.T.— 6th hy. art.

COW CREEK, KAN.
(Nov. 14, 1864)
U.S.C.T.— 54th inf.

COX'S BRIDGE, N.C.
(March 24, 1865)
U.S.C.T.— 30th inf.

DALLAS, GA.
(May 31, 1864)
U.S.C.T.— 110th inf.

DALTON, GA.
(Aug. 15 and 16, 1864)
U.S.C.T.— 14th inf.

DARBYTOWN ROAD, VA.
(Oct. 13, 1864)
U.S.C.T.— 7th, 8th, 9th & 29th (Conn.) inf.

DAVIS' BEND, LA.
(June 2 and 29, 1864)
U.S.C.T.— 64th inf.

DECATUR, TENN.
(Aug. 18, 1864)
U.S.C.T.— 1st hy. art.

DECATUR, ALA.
(Oct. 28 and 29, 1864)
U.S.C.T.— 14th inf.

DECATUR, ALA.
(Dec. 27 and 28, 1864)
U.S.C.T.— 17th inf.

DEEP BOTTOM, VA.
(Aug. 14 to 18, 1864)
U.S.C.T.— 7th and 9th inf.

DEEP BOTTOM, VA.
(Sept. 2 and 6, 1864)
U.S.C.T.— 2d cav.

DEEP BOTTOM, VA.
(Oct. 1, 1864)
U.S.C.T.— 38th inf.

DEEP BOTTOM, VA.
(Oct. 31, 1864)
U.S.C.T.— 127th inf.

DEVEAUX NECK, S.C.
(Dec. 7, 8, and 9, 1864)
U.S.C.T.— 32d, 34th, 55th (Mass.) and 102d inf.

DRURY'S BLUFF, VA.
(May 10, 16, and 20, 1864)
U.S.C.T.— 2d cav.

DUTCH GAP, VA.
(Aug. 24, 1864)
U.S.C.T.— 22d inf.

DUTCH GAP, VA.
(Sept. 7, 1864)
U.S.C.T.— 4th inf.

DUTCH GAP, VA.
(Nov. 17, 1864)
U.S.C.T.— 36th inf.

EAST PASCAGOULA, MISS.
(April 9, 1863)
U.S.C.T.— Cos. B and C, 74th inf.

EASTPORT, MISS.
(Oct. 10, 1864)
U.S.C.T.— 61st inf.

FAIR OAKS, VA.
(Oct. 27 and 28, 1864)
U.S.C.T.— 1st, 5th, 9th, 22d, 29th (Conn.) and 37th inf.

FEDERAL POINT, N.C.
(Feb. 11, 1865)
U.S.C.T.— 39th inf.

FILLMORE, VA.
(Oct. 4, 1864)
U.S.C.T.— 1st inf.

FLOYD, LA.
(July--, 1864)
U.S.C.T.— 51st inf.

FORT ADAMS, LA.
(Oct. 5, 1864)
U.S.C.T.— 3d cav.

FORT ANDERSON, KY.
(March 25, 1864)
U.S.C.T.— 8th hy. art.

FORT BLAKELY, ALA.
(March 31 to April 9, 1865)
U.S.C.T.— 47th, 48th, 50th, 51st, 68th, 73d, 76th, 82d, and 86th inf.

FORT BRADY, VA.
(Jan. 24, 1865)
U.S.C.T.— 118th inf.

FORT BURNHAM, VA.
(Dec. 10, 1864)
U.S.C.T.— 41st inf.

FORT BURNHAM, VA.
(Jan. 24, 1865)
U.S.C.T.— 7th inf.

FORT DONELSON, TENN.
(Oct. 11, 1864)
U.S.C.T.— 4th hy. art.

FORT GAINES, ALA.
(Aug. 2 to 8, 1864)
U.S.C.T.— 96th inf.

FORT GIBSON, C.N.
(Sept. 16, 1864)
U.S.C.T.— 79th (new) inf.

FORT GIBSON, C.N.
(Sept.--, 1865)
U.S.C.T.— 54th inf.

FORT JONES, KY.
(Feb. 18, 1865)
U.S.C.T.— 12th hy. art.

FORT PILLOW, TENN.
(April 12, 1864)
U.S.C.T.— Batt'y F, 2d lt. art.; 11th (new) inf.

FORT POCAHONTAS, VA.
(Aug.--, 1864)
U.S.C.T.— 1st cav.

FORT SMITH, ARK.
(Aug. 24, 1864)
U.S.C.T.— 11th (old) inf.

FORT SMITH, ARK.
(Dec. 24, 1864)
U.S.C.T.— 83d (new) inf.

FORT TAYLOR, FLA.
(Aug. 21, 1864)
U.S.C.T.— 2d inf.

FORT WAGNER, S.C.
(July 18 and Sept. 6, 1863)
U.S.C.T.— 54th (Mass.) inf.

FORT WAGNER, S.C.
(Aug. 26, 1863)
U.S.C.T.— 3d inf.

FRANKLIN, MISS.
(Jan. 2, 1865)
U.S.C.T.— 3d cav.

GHENT, KY.
(Aug. 29, 1864)
U.S.C.T.— 117th inf.

GLASGOW, MO.
(Oct. 15, 1864)
U.S.C.T.— 62d inf.

GLASGOW, KY.
(March 25, 1863)
U.S.C.T.— 119th inf.

GOODRICH'S LANDING, LA.
(March 24 and July 16, 1864)
U.S.C.T.— 66th inf.

GRAND GULF, MISS.
(July 16, 1864)
U.S.C.T.— 53d inf.

GREGORY'S FARM, S.C.
(Dec. 5 and 9, 1864)
U.S.C.T.— 26th inf.

HALL ISLAND, S.C.
(Nov. 24, 1863)
U.S.C.T.— 33d inf.

HARRODSBURG, KY.
(Oct. 21, 1864)
U.S.C.T.— 5th cav.

HATCHER'S RUN, VA.
(Oct. 27 and 28, 1864)
U.S.C.T.— 27th, 39th, 41st, 43d and 45th inf.

HAYNES' BLUFF, MISS.
(Feb. 3, 1864)
U.S.C.T.— 53d inf.

HAYNES' BLUFF, MISS.
(April--, 1864)
U.S.C.T.— 3d cav.

HELENA, ARK.
(Aug. 2, 1864)
U.S.C.T.— 64th inf.

HENDERSON, KY.
(Sept. 25, 1864)
U.S.C.T.— 118th inf.

HOLLY SPRINGS, MISS.
(Aug. 28, 1864)
U.S.C.T.— 11th (new) inf.

HONEY HILL, S.C.
(Nov. 30, 1864)
U.S.C.T.— 32d, 35th, 54th and 55th (Mass.,) and 102nd inf.

HONEY SPRING, I.T.
(July 17, 1863)
U.S.C.T.— 79th (new) inf.

HOPKINSVILLE, VA.
(Dec. 12, 1864)
U.S.C.T.— 5th cav.

HORSE-HEAD CREEK, ARK.
(Feb. 17, 1864)
U.S.C.T.— 79th (new) inf.

INDIAN BAY, ARK.
(April 13, 1864)
U.S.C.T.— 56th inf.

INDIANTOWN, N.C.
(Dec. 18, 1863)
U.S.C.T.— 36th inf.

INDIAN VILLAGE, LA.
(Aug. 6, 1864)
U.S.C.T.— 11th hy. art.

ISLAND MOUND, MO.
(Oct. 27 and 29, 1862)
U.S.C.T.— 79th (new) inf.

ISLAND NO. 76, MISS.
(Jan. 20, 1864)
U.S.C.T.— Batt'y E, 2d lt. art.

ISSEQUENA COUNTY, MISS.
(July 10 and Aug. 17, 1864)
U.S.C.T.— 66th inf.

JACKSON, LA.
(Aug. 3, 1863)
U.S.C.T.— 73d, 75th, and 78th inf.

JACKSON, MISS.
(July 5, 1864)
U.S.C.T.— 3d cav.

JACKSONVILLE, FLA.
(March 29, 1863)
U.S.C.T.— 33d inf.

JACKSONVILLE, FLA.
(May 1 and 28, 1864)
U.S.C.T.— 7th inf.

JACKSONVILLE, FLA.
(April 4, 1865)
U.S.C.T.— 3d inf.

JAMES ISLAND, S.C.
(July 16, 1863)
U.S.C.T.— 54th (Mass.) inf.

JAMES ISLAND, S.C.
(May 21, 1864)
U.S.C.T.— 55th (Mass.) inf.

JAMES ISLAND, S.C.
(July 1 and 2, 1864)
U.S.C.T.— 33d, and 55th (Mass.) inf.

JAMES ISLAND, S.C.
(July 5 and 7, 1864)
U.S.C.T.— 7th inf.

JAMES ISLAND, S.C.
(Feb. 10, 1865)
U.S.C.T.— 55th (Mass.) inf.

JENKINS' FERRY, ARK.
(April 30, 1864)
U.S.C.T.— 79th (new) and 83d (new) inf.

JENKINS' FERRY, ARK.
(May 4, 1864)
U.S.C.T.— 83d (new) inf.

JOHN'S ISLAND, S.C.
(July 5 and 7, 1864)
U.S.C.T.— 26th inf.

JOHN'S ISLAND, S.C.
(July 9, 1864)
U.S.C.T.— 7th and 34th inf.

JOHNSONVILLE, TENN.
(Sept. 25, 1864)
U.S.C.T.— 13th inf.

JONES' BRIDGE, VA.
(June 23, 1864)
U.S.C.T.— 28th inf.

JOY'S FORD, ARK.
(Jan. 8, 1865)
U.S.C.T.— 79th (new) inf.

LAKE PROVIDENCE, LA.
(May 27, 1863)
U.S.C.T.— 47th inf.

LAWRENCE, KAN.
(July 27, 1863)
U.S.C.T.— 79th (new) inf.

LITTLE ROCK, ARK.
(April 26 and May 28, 1864)
U.S.C.T.— 57th inf.

LIVERPOOL HEIGHTS, MISS.
(Feb. 3, 1864)
U.S.C.T.— 47th inf.

"LOTUS" STEAMER, ARK.
(Jan. 17, 1865)
U.S.C.T.— 83d (new) inf.

MADISON STATION, ALA.
(Nov. 26, 1864)
U.S.C.T.— 101st inf.

MAGNOLIA, TENN.
(Jan. 7, 1865)
U.S.C.T.— 15th inf.

MARIANA, FLA.
(Sept. 27, 1864)
U.S.C.T.— 82nd inf.

MARION, VA.
(Dec. 18, 1864)
U.S.C.T.— 6th cav.

MARION COUNTY, FLA.
(March 10, 1865)
U.S.C.T.— 3d inf.

McKAY'S POINT, S.C.
(Dec. 22, 1864)
U.S.C.T.— 26th inf.

MEFFLETON LODGE, ARK.
(June 29, 1864)
U.S.C.T.— 56th inf.

MEMPHIS, TENN.
(Aug. 21, 1864)
U.S.C.T.— 61st inf.

MILLIKEN'S BEND, LA.
(June 5,6, and 7, 1863)
U.S.C.T.— 5th hy. art.; 49th and 51st inf.

MILLTOWN BLUFF, S.C.
(July 10, 1863)
U.S.C.T.— 33d inf.

MITCHELL'S CREEK, FLA.
(Dec. 17, 1864)
U.S.C.T.— 82d inf.

MORGANZIA, LA.
(May 18, 1864)
U.S.C.T.— 73d inf.

MORGANZIA, LA.
(Nov. 23, 1864)
U.S.C.T.— 84th inf.

MOSCOW, TENN.
(June 15, 1864)
U.S.C.T.— 55th inf.

MOSCOW STATION, TENN.
(Dec. 4, 1863)
U.S.C.T.— 61st inf.

MOUND PLANTATION, LA.
(June 29, 1863)
U.S.C.T.— 46th inf.

MOUNT PLEASANT LANDING, LA.
(May 15, 1864)
U.S.C.T.— 67th inf.

MUD CREEK, ALA.
(Jan. 5, 1865)
U.S.C.T.— 106th inf.

MURFREESBORO, TENN.
(Dec. 24, 1864)
U.S.C.T.— 12th inf.

N. AND N. W. R.R., TENN.
(Sept. 4, 1864)
U.S.C.T.— 100th inf.

NASHVILLE, TENN.
(May 24, 1864)
U.S.C.T.— 15th inf.

NASHVILLE, TENN.
(Dec. 2 and 21, 1864)
U.S.C.T.— 44th inf.

NASHVILLE, TENN.
(Dec. 7, 1864)
U.S.C.T.— 18th inf.

NASHVILLE, TENN.
(Dec. 15 and 16, 1864)
U.S.C.T.— 12th, 13th, 14th, 17th, 18th and 100th inf.

NATCHEZ, MISS.
(Nov. 11, 1863)
U.S.C.T.— 58th inf.

NATCHEZ, MISS.
(April 25, 1864)
U.S.C.T.— 98th inf.

NATURAL BRIDGE, FLA.
(March 6, 1865)
U.S.C.T.— 2d and 99th inf.

NEW KENT COURT HOUSE, VA.
(March 2, 1864)
U.S.C.T.— 5th inf.

NEW MARKET HEIGHTS, VA.
(June 24, 1864)
U.S.C.T.— 22d inf.

OLUSTEE, FLA.
(Feb. 20, 1864)
U.S.C.T.— 8th and 35th, and 54th (Mass.) inf.

OWENSBORO,KY.
(Aug. 27, 1864)
U.S.C.T.— 108th inf.

PALMETTO RANCH, TEXAS
(May 15, 1865)
U.S.C.T.— 62d inf.

PASS MANCHAS, LA.
(March 20, 1864)
U.S.C.T.— 10th hy. art.

PETERSBURG, VA.
(June 15, 1864 to April 2, 1865)
U.S.C.T.— 5th (Mass.) cav.; 1st, 4th, 5th, 6th, 7th, 10th, 19th, 22d, 23d, 27th, 28th, 29th, 29th (Conn.,) 30th, 31st, 36th, 39th, 41st, 43d, 45th, and 116th inf.

PIERSON'S FARM, VA.
(June 16, 1864)
U.S.C.T.— 36th inf.

PINE BARREN CREEK, ALA.
(Dec. 17, 18, and 19, 1864)
U.S.C.T.— 97th inf.

PINE BARREN FORD, FLA.
(Dec. 17 and 18, 1864)
U.S.C.T.— 82d inf.

PINE BLUFF, ARK.
(July 2, 1864)
U.S.C.T.— 64th inf.

PLEASANT HILL, LA.
(April 9, 1864)
U.S.C.T.— 75th inf.

PLYMOUTH, N.C.
(Nov. 26, 1863 and April 18, 1864)
U.S.C.T.— 10th inf.

PLYMOUTH, N.C.
(April 1, 1864)
U.S.C.T.— 37th inf.

POINT LOOKOUT, VA.
(May 13, 1864)
U.S.C.T.— 36th inf.

POINT OF ROCKS, MD.
(June 9, 1864)
U.S.C.T.— 2d cav.

POINT PLEASANT, LA.
(June 25, 1864)
U.S.C.T.— 64th inf.

POISON SPRINGS, ARK.
(April 18, 1864)
U.S.C.T.— 79th (new) inf.

PORT HUDSON, LA.
(May 22 to July 8, 1863)
U.S.C.T.— 73d, 75th, 78th, 79th (old) 80th, 81st, 82d, and 95th inf.

POWHATAN, VA.
(Jan. 25, 1865)
U.S.C.T.— 1st cav.

PRAIRIE D'ANN, ARK.
(April 13, 1864)
U.S.C.T.— 79th (new) and 83d (new) inf.

PULASKI, TENN.
(May 13, 1864)
U.S.C.T.— 111th inf.

RALEIGH, N.C.
(April 7, 1865)
U.S.C.T.— 5th inf.

RECTOR'S FARM, ARK.
(Dec. 19, 1864)
U.S.C.T.— 83d (new) inf.

RED RIVER EXPEDITION, LA.
(May--, 1864)
U.S.C.T.— 92d inf.

RICHLAND, TENN.
(Sept. 26, 1864)
U.S.C.T.— 111th inf.

RICHMOND, VA.
(Oct. 28 and 29, 1864)
U.S.C.T.— 2d cav.; 7th inf.

RIPLEY, MISS.
(June 7, 1864)
U.S.C.T.— 55th inf.

ROACHE'S PLANTATION, MISS.
(March 31, 1864)
U.S.C.T.— 3d cav.

ROLLING FORK, MISS.
(Nov. 22, 1864)
U.S.C.T.— 3d cav.

ROSEVILLE CREEK, ARK.
(March 20, 1864)
U.S.C.T.— 79th (new) inf.

ROSS' LANDING, ARK.
(Feb. 14, 1864)
U.S.C.T.— 51st inf.

ST. JOHN'S RIVER, S.C.
(May 23, 1864)
U.S.C.T.— 35th inf.

ST. STEPHEN'S S.C.
(March 1, 1865)
U.S.C.T.— 55th (Mass.) inf.

SALINE RIVER, ARK.
(May 4, 1864)
U.S.C.T.— 83d (new) inf.

SALINE RIVER, ARK.
(May--, 1865)
U.S.C.T.— 54th inf.

SALKEHATCHIE, S.C.
(Feb. 9, 1865)
U.S.C.T.— 102d inf.

SALTVILLE, VA.
(Oct. 2, 1864)
U.S.C.T.— 5th and 6th cav.

SALTVILLE, VA.
(Dec. 20, 1864)
U.S.C.T.— 5th cav.

SAND MOUNTAIN, TENN.
(Jan. 27, 1865)
U.S.C.T.— 18th inf.

SANDY SWAMP, N.C.
(Dec. 18, 1863)
U.S.C.T.— 5th inf.

SCOTTSBORO, ALA.
(Jan. 8, 1865)
U.S.C.T.— 101st inf.

SECTION 37, N. AND N.W.R.R., TENN.
(Nov. 24, 1864)
U.S.C.T.— 12th inf.

SHERWOOD,MO.
(May 18, 1863)
U.S.C.T.— 79th (new) inf.

SIMPSONVILLE, KY.
(Jan. 25, 1865)
U.S.C.T.— 5th cav.

SMITHFIELD, VA.
(Aug. 30, 1864)
U.S.C.T.— 1st cav.

SMITHFIELD, KY.
(Jan. 5, 1865)
U.S.C.T.— 6th cav.

SOUTH TUNNEL, TENN.
(Oct. 10, 1864)
U.S.C.T.— 40th inf.

SPANISH FORT, ALA.
(March 27 to April 8, 1865)
U.S.C.T.— 68th inf.

SUFFOLK, VA.
(March 9, 1864)
U.S.C.T.— 2d cav.

SUGAR LOAF HILL, N.C.
(Jan. 19, 1865)
U.S.C.T.— 6th inf.

SUGAR LOAF HILL, N.C.
(Feb. 11, 1865)
U.S.C.T.— 4th, 6th, and 30th inf.

SULPHUR BRANCH TRESTLE, ALA.
(Sept. 25, 1864)
U.S.C.T.— 111th inf.

SWIFT'S CREEK, S.C.
(April 19, 1865)
U.S.C.T.— 102d inf.

TAYLORSVILLE, KY.
(April 18, 1865)
U.S.C.T.— 119th inf.

TIMBER HILL, C.N.
(Nov. 19, 1864)
U.S.C.T.— 79th (new) inf.

TOWN CREEK, N.C.
(Feb. 20, 1865)
U.S.C.T.— 1st inf.

TOWNSHIP, FLA.
(Jan. 26, 1863)
U.S.C.T.— 33d inf.

TUPELO, MISS.
(July 13, 14, and 15, 1864)
U.S.C.T.— 59th, 61st, and 68th inf.

VICKSBURG, MISS.
(Aug. 27, 1863)
U.S.C.T.— 5th hy. art.

VICKSBURG, MISS.
(Feb. 13, 1864)
U.S.C.T.— 52d inf.

VICKSBURG, MISS.
(June 4, 1864)
U.S.C.T.— 3d cav.

VICKSBURG, MISS.
(July 4, 1864)
U.S.C.T.— 48th inf.

VIDALIA, LA.
(July 22, 1864)
U.S.C.T.— 6th hy. art.

WALLACE'S FERRY, ARK.
(July 26, 1864)
U.S.C.T.— 56th inf.

WARSAW, N.C.
(April 6, 1865)
U.S.C.T.— 1st inf.

WATERFORD, MISS.
(Aug. 16 and 17, 1864)
U.S.C.T.— 55th and 61st inf.

WATERLOO, LA.
(Oct. 20, 1864)
U.S.C.T.— 75th inf.

WATERPROOF, LA.
(Feb. 14, 1864)
U.S.C.T.— 49th inf.

WATERPROOF, LA.
(April 20, 1864)
U.S.C.T. — 63d inf.

WHITE OAK ROAD, VA.
(March 31, 1865)
U.S.C.T.— 29th inf.

WHITE RIVER, ARK.
(Oct. 22, 1864)
U.S.C.T.— 53d inf.

WILLIAMSBURG, VA.
(March 4, 1864)
U.S.C.T.— 6th inf.

WILMINGTON, N.C.
(Feb. 22, 1865)
U.S.C.T.— 1st inf.

WILSON'S LANDING, VA.
(June 11, 1864)
U.S.C.T.— 1st cav.

WILSON'S WHARF, VA.
(May 24, 1864)
U.S.C.T.— Batt'y B, 2d lt. art.; 1st and 10th inf.

YAZOO CITY, MISS.
(March 5, 1864)
U.S.C.T.— 3d cav.; 47th inf.

YAZOO CITY, MISS.
(May 13, 1864)
U.S.C.T.— 3d cav.

YAZOO CITY, MISS.
(March 15, 1865)
U.S.C.T.— 3d cav.

YAZOO EXPEDITION, MISS.
(Feb. 28, 1864)
U.S.C.T.— 3d cav.

Note: for a more complete listing of the skirmishes, engagements and battles of the U.S. Colored Troops consult Frederick Dyers' *A Compendium of the War of the Rebellion.* Dyer listed the final designation of the colored regiment which might not have been the numerical designation of the regiment participating in the battle.

APPENDIX VIII

Regiments of United States Colored Troops that lost fifty or more in killed or mortally wounded during the Civil War.*

Regiment	Officers	Enlisted Men	Total
1st USCT	4	67	71
4th USCT	3	102	105
5th USCT	4	77	81
6th USCT	8	79	87
7th USCT	1	84	85
8th USCT	4	115	119
13th USCT	4	86	90
19th USCT	3	47	50
22nd USCT	2	70	72
23rd USCT	4	82	86
31st USCT	3	48	51
35th USCT	4	49	53
43rd USCT	3	48	51
49th USCT	3	59	62
79th USCT	5	183	188

*Dyer, Frederick H. *A Compendium of the War of the Rebellion.*

APPENDIX IX

Effective Strength of the U.S.C.T. Regiments per Annual Loss per 1,000 men

For many years after the war the U.S. Army did a number of studies on the performance of the classes of troops serving during the Civil War. The performance of Colored Troops surpassed those of the Regular Army and Volunteers. The same study segregated the colored soldier from the white soldier with respect to the number of men effective in every thousand of mean aggregate strength.*

Absent per 1,000 men	
Colored	158
White	264
Mixed	258
Regulars	226
Volunteers	265

Sick in Hospital per 1,000 men	
Colored	46
White	86
Mixed	80
Regulars	64
Volunteers	89

Consequent effective strength per 1,000 of troops concerned	
Colored	796
White	650
Mixed	662
Regulars	710
Volunteers	646

General Mortality, Annual loss per 1,000 men	
Colored	176.3
White	74.6
Mixed	79.7
Regulars	47.6
Volunteers	75.4

Killed in Battle, Annual loss per 1,000 men	
Colored	10.6
White	18.9
Mixed	18.4
Regulars	19.9
Volunteers	18.8

Died of Wounds, Annual loss per 1,000 men	
Colored	10.8
White	11.2
Mixed	10.8
Regulars	11.7
Volunteers	11.2

Total loss by death, Annual loss per 1,000 men	
Colored	197.7
White	104.7
Mixed	108.9
Regulars	79.2
Volunteers	105.4

*Phisterer, Frederick. *Statistical Record of the Armies of the United States.*

APPENDIX X

Number of Colored Troops furnished by the States and District of Columbia.*

Connecticut	1,764
Delaware	954
District of Columbia	3,269
Illinois	1,811
Indiana	1,537
Iowa	440
Kansas	2,080
Kentucky	23,703
Maine	104
Maryland	8,718
Massachusetts	3,966
Michigan	1,387
Minnesota	104
Missouri	8,344
New Hampshire	125
New Jersey	1,185
New York	4,125
Ohio	5,092
Pennsylvania	8,612
Rhode Island	1,837
Vermont	120
West Virginia	196
Wisconsin	165
	79,638

The following colored soldiers were organized under the direct authority of the General Government and not credited to any state.*

Alabama	4,969
Arkansas	5,526
Colorado	95
Florida	1,044
Georgia	3,486
Louisiana	24,052
Mississippi	17,869
North Carolina	5,035
South Carolina	5,462
Tennessee	20,133
Texas	47
Virginia	5,723
At large	5,896
	99,337

Mustered in by Federal authority	99,337	
Mustered in by State Authority	79,638	
	178,975	Total Colored Soldiers Federal Service

*Fox, William L., *Regimental Losses in the American Civil War, 1861-1865.*

APPENDIX XI

Deaths in the United States Colored Troops during the War of the Rebellion in the records of the Adjutant General's Office.*

	Non-Prisoners		Prisoners	
	Officers	Enlisted	Officers	Enlisted
Killed in Action	100	1,615		
Died of Wounds received in Action	43	1,102		34
Died of Disease	137	29,521	1	97
Accidental Deaths	14	266		1
Drowned	6	288		1
Murdered	8	98		
Killed after capture			4	21
Committed suicide	2	11		
Executed by U.S. Military authorities		52		
Executed by the enemy			1	
Died from Sunstroke		32		
Other known causes	5	73		8
Causes not stated	2	3,181	1	122
	317	36,239	7	284

* Dyer, Frederick H., *A Compendium of the War of the Rebellion.*

APPENDIX XII

Colored sailors in the United States Navy.

The U.S. Navy was authorized to enlist "contrabands" for naval services as of September 25, 1861, under the same forms and regulations that applied to other enlistments. They were allowed no higher rating than boys, at a compensation of $10 per month and one ration a day.

There were 9,596 African-American sailors in the Civil War. Aboard ship they were integrated. Some of the first nurses aboard the hospital ship the U.S.S. Red Rover were of African descent.

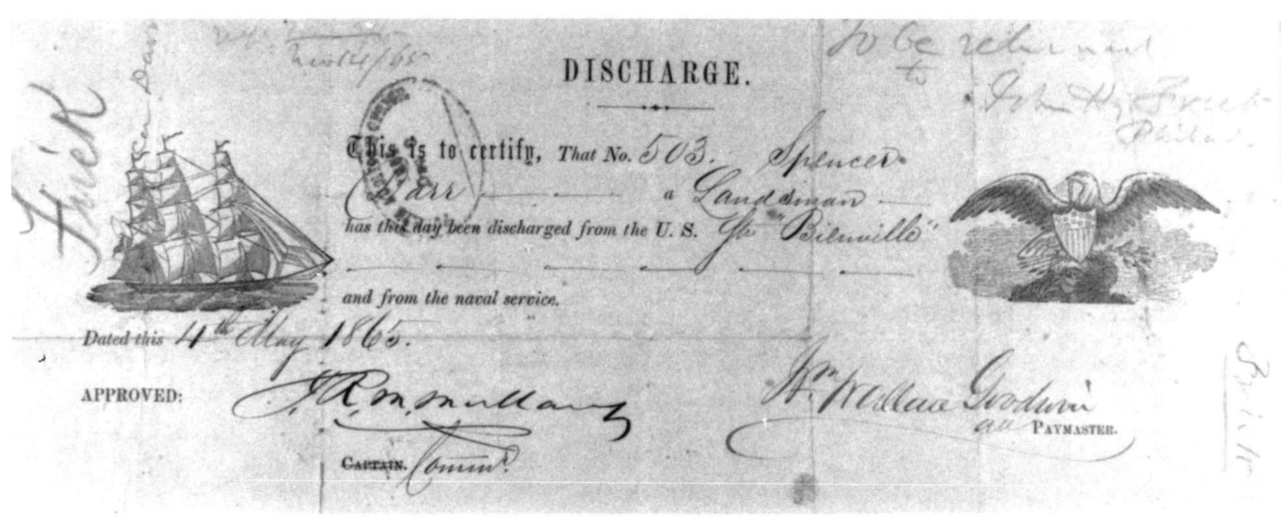

DISCHARGE.

This is to certify, That No. 503. Spencer Barr a Landsman has this day been discharged from the U. S. Str "Bienville" and from the naval service.

Dated this 4th May 1865.

APPROVED: [illegible]

Captain. Comm'd.

Wm Wallace Goodwin
Act Paymaster.

Landsman Stephen Barr was discharged for disability on May 4, 1866. The enlistment for colored sailors was for a period of one year.

The U.S. Navy had accepted colored sailors before the Army did. They also recognized the heroic deeds of their colored sailors by awarding the Medal of Honor about a year before the Army awarded its Medal of Honor.

Cased Navy Medal of Honor. The following is a list of the colored sailors in the U.S. Navy during the Civil War who earned the Medal of Honor. Seven of the eight soldiers received their medal, but Clement Dees deserted before he received the award.

U.S. Navy Medal of Honor

	Enlisted Men	*Rank*	*Date of Issue*
1.	Anderson, Aaron	Landsman	June 22, 1865
2.	Blake, Robert	Landsman	April 16, 1864
3.	Brown, William H.	Landsman	August 5, 1864
4.	Brown, Wilson	Landsman	December 31, 1864
5.	Dees, Clement	Seaman	
6.	Lawson, John	Landsman	December 31, 1864
7.	Mifflin, James	Engineer's Cook	August 5, 1864
8.	Pease, Joachim	Seaman	December 31, 1864

APPENDIX XIII

BIBLIOGRAPHY and SUGGESTED READING

Andrews, C. C. *History of the Campaign of Mobile; Including the Cooperative Operations of Gen. Wilson's Cavalry in Alabama.* New York: D. Van Nostrand, 1889.

Bahney, Robert Stanley. *Generals and Negroes: Education of Negroes by the Union Army, 1861-1865.* Ann Arbor, Mich.: University Microfilms; unpublished dissertation, Univ. of Michigan, 1965.

Baird, George W. *The 32d Regiment, U.S.C.T. at the Battle of Honey Hill.* n.p., [1889].

Bates, Samuel P. *History of Pennsylvania Volunteers 1861-1865.* 5 volumes. Harrisburg, 1869-1871.

Beatty, John. *The Citizen-Soldier; or, Memoirs of a Volunteer.* Cincinnati: Wilstach, Baldwin and Co., 1879.

Berlin, Ira et al, Editors. *Freedom: A Documentary History of Emancipation, 1861-1867, Series II, The Black Military Experience.* London: Cambridge University Press, 1982.

Berry, Mary Frances. *Military Necessity and Civil Rights Policy: Black Citizenship and the Constitution, 1861-1868.* Port Washington, NY: Kennikat Press, 1977.

Binder, Frederick M. "Pennsylvania Negro Regiments in the Civil War," *Journal of Negro History,* Vol. 37, October, 1952, pp. 383-417.

Blassingame, John W. "Negro Chaplains in the Civil War," *Negro History Bulletin,* Vol. 27, October, 1963, pp. 23-24.

________________. "The Freedom Fighters," *Negro History Bulletin,* Vol. 28, February, 1965, pp. 105-106.

________________. "The Organization and Use of Negro Troops in the Union Army, 1863-1865." Unpublished Master's Thesis, Howard University, 1961.

________________. "The Recruitment of Colored Troops in Kentucky, Maryland and Missouri, 1863-1865," *The Historian,* 1967, pp. 533-545.

________________. "The Selection of Officers and Non-Commissioned Officers of Negro Troops in the Union Army, 1863-1865," *Negro History Bulletin,* Vol. 30, January, 1967, pp. 8-11.

________________. "The Union Army as an Educational Institution for Negroes, 1862-1865," *Journal of Negro Education,* Vol. 34, Spring, 1965, pp. 152-159.

Brewer, James H. *The Confederate Negro: Virginia's Craftsmen and Military Laborers, 1861-1865.* Durham, N.C.: Duke Univ. Press, 1969.

Brown, William Wells. *The Negro in the American Rebellion, His Heroism and His Fidelity.* Boston: Lee and Shepard, 1867.

Browne, Frederick W. *My Service in the U.S. Colored Cavalry.* Cincinnati: Ohio Commandery of the Loyal Legion, 1908.

Burchard, Peter. *One Gallant Rush: Robert Gould Shaw and His Brave Black Regiment.* New York: St. Martin's Press, 1965.

Butler, Benjamin F. *Butler's Book.* Boston: A.M. Thayer and Co., 1892.

[Califf, J.M.]. *Record of the Services of the Seventh Regiment, U.S. Colored Troops, from September, 1863, to November, 1866.* Providence, R.I.: E.L. Freeman and Co., 1878.

Chase, Salmon P. *Inside Lincoln's Cabinet.* Edited by David Donald. New York: Longmans, Green and Co., 1954.

Chenery, William H. *The Fourteenth Regiment Rhode Island Heavy Artillery (Colored) in the War to Preserve the Union, 1861-1865.* Providence, R.I.: Snow and Farnham, 1898.

Clark, Peter H. *The Black Brigade of Cincinnati: Being a Report of its Labors and a Muster-Roll of its Members...* Cincinnati, O.: Joseph B. Boyd, printer, 1864.

Cochrane, John. *Arming the Slaves in the War for the Union.* New York: Rogers and Sherwood, 1875.

Confederate States of America. Congress. *Journal of the Congress of the Confederate States of America, 1861-1865,* 7 vols. Washington, D.C.: GPO, 1904.

Cornish, Dudley Taylor. *The Sable Arm: Negro Troops in the Union Army, 1861-1865.* New York: Longmans, Green and Co., 1956.

Cowden, Robert. *A Brief Sketch of the Organization and Services of the Fifty-Ninth Regiment of United States Colored Infantry, and Biographical Sketches.* Dayton, Ohio: United Brethren Publishing House, 1883.

Dennett, George M. *History of the Ninth U.S.C. Troops...* Philadelphia: King and Baird, 1866.

Drinkard, Dorothy Lee. *A Regiment History of the Twenty-Ninth Infantry, United States Colored Regiments, 1864-1865.* Washington, DC: Howard University, 1963.

Dyer, Frederick H. *A Compendium of the War of the Rebellion.* Dayton, OH: Morningside Bookshop, 1978.

Emilio, Luis F. *The Assault on Fort Wagner, July 18, 1863: The Memorable Charge of the Fifty-Fourth Regiment of Massachusetts Volunteers.* Boston: Rand Avery Co., 1887.

______________. *A Brave Black Regiment: History of the Fifty-Fourth Regiment of Massachusetts Volunteer Infantry, 1863-1865.* New York: Arno Press, 1969; originally published 1894.

______________. *History of the Fifty-Fourth Regiment of Massachusetts Volunteer Infantry, 1863-1865.* Boston: Boston Book Co., 1894.

Fleetwood, Christian A. *The Negro As A Soldier.* Washington, D.C.: Howard Univ. Print, 1895.

Forty-Fourth Regiment U.S. Colored Troops. Gettysburg, PA: J.E. Wible, 1866.

Friends' Association of Philadelphia. *Statistics of the Operations of the Executive Board of Friends' Association of Philadelphia, and its Vicinity, for the Relief of Colored Freedmen,* 19 January 1864. Philadelphia: Inquirer Printing Office, [1864].

Hallowell, Norwood P. *The Negro as a Soldier in the War of the Rebellion.* Boston: Little, Brown, and Co., 1897.

Higginson, Thomas Wentworth. *Army Life in a Black Regiment.* Boston: Fields, Osgood, and Co., 1870.

Hill, Isaac J. *A Sketch of the 29th Regiment of Connecticut Colored Troops.* Baltimore: Daugherty, Maguire and Co., 1867.

Hunter, David. *Report of the Military Services of Gen. David Hunter, U.S.A.* ...New York: D. Van Nostrand, 1873.

Johnson, Robert, and Buel, Clarence, eds. *Battles and Leaders of the Civil War,* 4 vols. New York: The Century Co., 1887-1888.

Kautz, August V. *Reminiscences of the Civil War.* Typed manuscript, July 1936.

Kireker, Charles. *History of the 116th Regiment U.S.C. Infantry.* Philadelphia: King and Baird, 1866.

Knox, Thomas W. *Camp-Fire and Cotton-Field...* New York: Blelock and Co., 1865.

Lord, Francis A. *Civil War Sutlers and Their Wares.* A.S. Barnes and Co., 1969.

Main, Edwin M. *The Story of the Marches, Battles and Incidents of the Third United States Colored Cavalry, a Fighting Regiment in the War of the Rebellion, 1861-1865. With Official Orders and Reports Relating Thereto, Compiled from the Rebellion Records.* by Ed. M. Main, Late Major, New Orleans, Louisiana. Louisville, KY: Globe Printing Co., 1908.

Matson, Dan. "The Colored Man in the Civil War." *War Sketches and Incidents...,* vol. 2. Des Moines, Iowa: The Kenyon Press, 1898.

McConnell, Roland C. *Negro Troops of Antebellum Louisiana: A History of the Battalion of Free Men of Color.* Baton Rouge, LA: Louisiana State University Press, 1968.

McPherson, James M. *Marching Toward Freedom: The Negro in the Civil War, 1861-1865.* New York: Alfred A. Knopf, 1967.

______________. *The Negro's Civil War.* New York: Pantheon Books, 1965.

Meyer, Howard N. *Colonel of the Black Regiment: The Life of Thomas Wentworth Higginson.*

Michigan. Adjutant General's Office. *Record of Service of Michigan Volunteers in the Civil War 1861-1865: First Colored Infantry.* Kalamazoo, Mich.: Mich. Legislature, n.d.

Mickley, Jeremiah Marion. *The Forty-Third Regiment United States Colored Troops.* Gettysburg: J.E. Wible, 1866.

Moore, Frank, ed. *The Rebellion Record: A Diary of American Events,* 11 vols. New York: D. Van Nostrand, 1861-1868.

Newton, Alexander Herritage. *Out of the Briars: An Autobiography and Sketch of the Twenty-Ninth Regiment Connecticut Volunteers*. Philadelphia: A.M.E. Book Concern, 1910.

New York Association for Colored Volunteers. *First Organization of Colored Troops in the State of New York*. New York: Baker and Bodwin, 1864.

Norton, Henry Allyn. "Colored Troops in the War of the Rebellion," *Glimpse of the Nation's Struggle*. St. Paul, MN: Review Publishing Co., 1903.

Norton, Oliver Wilcox, *Army Letters, 1861-1865*. Chicago: O.L. Deming, 1903.

Parton, James. *General Butler in New Orleans: History of the Administration of the Department of the Gulf in the Year 1862*. New York: Mason Bros., 1864.

Phisterer, Frederick. *Statistical Record of the Armies of the United States*. Charles Scribner's Sons, 1883.

Rollin, Frank A. *Life and Public Services of Martin R. Delany*...Boston: Lee and Shephard, 1868.

Seraile, William. "New York's Black Regiments During the Civil War." Unpublished Doctoral Dissertation, City University of New York, 1977.

Taggart, John H. *Free Military School for Applicants for Command of Colored Troops*. Philadelphia: King and Baird, 1864.

Taylor, Frank H. *Philadelphia in the Civil War 1861-1865*. Philadelphia, 1913.

Taylor, Susie King. *Reminiscences of My Life in Camp*. New York: Arno Press, 1968; originally published 1902.

Todd, Frederick P. *American Military Equipage 1851-1872, Volume II—State Forces*. Chatham Square Press, 1983.

Trowbridge, Charles Tyler. "Six Months in the Freedmen's Bureau with a Colored Regiment." *Glimpses of the Nation's Struggle*, vol. 6. Minneapolis, Minn.: Aug. Davis, Publisher, 1909. pp. 198-222.

U.S. Army. War College. Historical Section. *The Colored Soldier in the United States Army*.

U.S. Congress. Joint Committee on the Conduct of the War. *Report*. 38th Cong., 1st sess. Sen. Rep. Com. No. 63 and 68. Washington, D.C.: n.p., 1864.

________________. *Report of the Committee...on the Attack on Petersburg, on the 30th Day of July, 1864*. 38th Cong., 2d sess., Sen. Rep. Com. No. 114. Washington, D.C.: GPO, 1865.

U.S. War Department. *Official Army Register of the Volunteer Force of the United States Army, 1861-65*, Part VIII, Washington: 1867.

________________. *U.S. Infantry Tactics...for the Use of the Colored Troops of the United States Infantry*. New York: D. Van Nostrand, 1863.

________________. *The War of the Rebellion: A Compilation of the Official Records of the Union and Confederate Armies*, 128 vols. Washington, D.C.: GPO, 1880-1901.

Voegeli, V. Jacque. *Free But Not Equal: The Midwest and the Negro During the Civil War*. Chicago: Univ. of Chicago Press, 1967.

Wallace, Andrew. *Gen. August V. Kautz and the Southwestern Frontier*. Tucson, Ariz.: Andrew Wallace, 1967.

INDEX